Contents

Part 1 Germany in defeat and 2
revolution
1 The Kaiser must go!   2
2 Abdication and revolution   4
3 Germany becomes a republic   7
4 The Republic under attack   10
5 The shock of Versailles   13
6 Occupation of the Ruhr   16
7 Germany's 'maddest year'   19

Part 2 The Nazis and Weimar 22
8 Hitler enters politics   22
9 Hitler: the public figure   24
10 Hitler: the private individual   26
11 The Hitler Putsch, November   28
1923
12 For and against the Putsch   30

Part 3 Weimar recovery 32
13 Germany and the Dawes   32
Plan
14 Locarno and the League,   34
1925–26
15 Weimar prosperity   36

Part 4 The Nazis re-organise, 38
1925–29
16 Hitler in Landsberg   38
17 The Fuehrer in waiting, 1925   40
18 The SA at work, 1926–29   42

Part 5 The Nazis win support, 45
1929–33
19 The Wall Street Crash and   45
economic crisis
20 The Nazi propaganda   47
machine
21 The Nazi breakthrough, 1930   50
22 The mass rallies   53
23 Masters of the streets   55
24 The respectable face of   58
Nazism
25 Why I became a Nazi   60

Part 6
26 The Reichstag fire, February
1933
27 The March elections, 1933   64
28 The Enabling Act, March   66
1933
29 Crushing the opposition, 1933   68
30 Night of the Long Knives,   70
1934

Part 7 The Nazi state 72
31 The Nazi state and the   72
workers
32 The Nazi state and women   74
33 The Nazi state and young   76
people
34 The Nazi state and education   79
35 The Nazi state and the   82
churches
36 The Nazi state and Jewish   85
people
37 'Crystal Night', November   88
1938
38 The Nazi terror machine   90
39 Resistance to Hitler   92

Part 8 Hitler and the 94
European War
40 Hitler's foreign policy goals   94
41 The Czech crisis, September   96
1938
42 Steps to war, 1938–39   98
43 The German war economy   100
44 The Jewish tragedy   102
45 The war is lost, 1945   106
46 The Nazi legacy: a stunned   109
survivor looks back

Part 1

Germany in defeat and revolution

1 The Kaiser must go!

At the beginning of October 1918, the German army leaders knew that the only way to avoid being overrun by the British, French and American Allies was to sign an armistice with them.

Ernst Toller was a young student at the time, after being invalided out of the Germany army. In 1933 his autobiography (Source A) described the mood in the army and the country in the last months of the war.

In November 1918, revolution broke out in many towns, as sailors and soldiers began to mutiny. There were many demands for the Kaiser to give up his throne. One was made by Philip Scheidemann, a leading socialist. On 9 November The Times *reported the reasons given by Kaiser Wilhelm for ignoring these demands (Source B).*

On the night of 8 November a general strike was called and it was clear that revolution might break out in Berlin itself. The head of the government, or Chancellor, Prince Max von Baden, telephoned the Kaiser at army headquarters at Spa in Belgium and begged him to abdicate (Source C).

A German soldiers and citizens

The rush to enlist was a thing of the past; nobody joined up voluntarily now. The young recruits, children almost, were lashed into some sort of enthusiasm by patriotic schoolmasters ... [There were] rumours that whole regiments had mutinied at the front, that Austria would soon drop out of the war, that women had been looting grocers' shops and bakers' shops up and down the country.

Germany was hungry. Eminent scientists proved that clay had the same food value as flour, that saccharine-sweetened jam was healthier than butter, that dried potato tops were better for the nerves than tobacco and tasted just as good. But the pronouncements of scientists were of little avail to the stomach, which reacted to their nonsense in its own way: people collapsed, fell sick, grew desperate.

From Ernst Toller, *If I was a German*, John Lane/Bodley Head, 1934.

B The Kaiser's refusal

Amsterdam, November 8. The *Lokalanseiger*, quoted by this morning's *Rheinisch-Westfälische Zeitung*, reports that the Minister of the Interior, Herr Drews, reported to the Kaiser on Herr Scheidemann's demand for the Kaiser's abdication. On returning from Headquarters, Herr Drews stated that his mission had been unsuccessful. The Kaiser, he said, declared that in view of the present disorganised state of affairs he would in no circumstances voluntarily vacate his position. He could not possibly, at the moment of the conclusion of peace, hand over Germany to the Entente. His abdication, the Kaiser further said, would produce complete anarchy and an augmentation of Bolshevist ideas. He would not assume responsibility for such a terrible state of affairs, and therefore would not, at the present moment, abdicate. REUTER

From *The Times*, 9 November 1918.

C Max von Baden talks to Wilhelm, 8 November 1918

Your abdication has become necessary to save Germany from civil war and to fulfil your mission as the Peacemaking Emperor till the end. The blood would be laid upon your head. The great majority of the people believes you to be responsible for the present situation. This belief is false, but it is held. If civil war and worse can be prevented through your abdication, your name will be blessed by future generations. . . . Disorders have already occurred. It might at first be possible to put them down by force, but once blood has flowed the cry for vengeance will everywhere be heard. The troops are not to be depended upon. . . . We are steering straight for civil war.

From *Memoirs of Prince Max von Baden*, Constable, 1928.

Questions

1 What signs of war-weariness can you find in Ernst Toller's account? Why might his report not be entirely reliable?

2 How would you describe the basic problem facing the home front by this time?

3 From *The Times* report, what did the Kaiser mean by not handing Germany over to the Entente? What two other reasons had he for not abdicating?

4 In which ways did Max von Baden view the situation differently from the Kaiser?

5 Do any of the sources give proof that the Kaiser was to blame for Germany's situation? How would you explain the demands for him to abdicate?

2 Abdication and revolution

On Saturday 9 November a general strike began in Berlin. Crowds marched towards the government buildings and soldiers did nothing to stop them. The Chancellor, Prince Max von Baden, feared a take-over by left-wing socialists linked to Lenin's Bolsheviks in the Soviet Union. To stop that happening he announced that the Kaiser had abdicated at 11.30 am.

Wilhelm did not hear of this for two hours. He protested, but his generals convinced him that the army could not be relied upon to support him, so in the early hours of the next morning Wilhelm left his headquarters in German-occupied Belgium in great secrecy for exile in Holland. Desperate to defend his actions, the Kaiser began work on his memoirs, which were published some three years later (Source A). Punch *magazine (Source B) portrayed the Kaiser's actions in a very different light.*

The rejoicing at his abdication and the scenes of revolution in Berlin on 9 November were seen by Princess Bluecher, a Lancashire woman who had married a German count in 1907. They lived in Britain until the war when they moved to Germany because public opinion was strongly hostile to 'aliens'. She kept a daily record of events and conversations to send to her mother which was published in 1920 (Source C).

A   The Kaiser's mental struggle

I went through a fearful mental struggle. On the one hand, I, as a soldier, was outraged at the idea of abandoning my still faithful, brave troops. On the other hand, there was the declaration of our foes that they were unwilling to conclude with me any peace endurable to Germany, as well as the statement of my own Government that only by my departure to foreign parts was civil war to be prevented.

After unspeakably arduous soul-struggles, and following the most urgent advice of my counsellors of the highest rank who were present at the moment, I decided to leave the country, for, in view of the reports made to me, I must needs believe that, by so doing, I should most faithfully serve Germany, make possible better armistice and peace terms for her, and spare her further loss of human life, distress and misery.

From Kaiser Wilhelm II, *My Memoirs 1878–1918*, Cassell, 1922.

From *Punch*, 11
December 1918.

WANTED.

WILLIAM THE GALLANT (*to Holland*). "COURAGE!   I WILL NEVER DESERT YOU."

C Berlin scenes: November 1918

At about two o'clock a perfect avalanche of humanity began to stream by our windows, walking quietly enough, many of them carrying red flags. I noticed the pale gold of young girls' uncovered heads as they passed by with only a shawl over their shoulders. It seemed so feminine and incongruous, under the folds of those gruesome red banners flying over them ... evidently no-one sorrowed at the loss of an emperor. There could hardly have been a greater air of rejoicing had Germany gained a great victory. More and more people came hurrying by, thousands of them densely packed together – men, women, soldiers, sailors and strangely enough, a never-ceasing fringe of children. .... A characteristic feature of the mob was the motors packed with youths in field-grey uniform or in civil clothes, carrying loaded rifles adorned with a tiny red flag, constantly springing off their seats and forcing the soldiers and officers to tear off their insignia, or doing it for them if they refused. They were mostly boys of from 16–18 years of age, who looked as though they were enjoying their sudden power immensely. .... I believe that any bloodshed that occurred was almost entirely due to the unrestrained freedom suddenly placed in their hands.

[A servant] tells me they made friends on the way with a young revolutionary soldier, who escorted them as a guard. He says he spoke so quietly and sensibly about the situation, saying they did not wish any bloodshed at all, but that they had been goaded by all the suffering and misery of the last four years spent in the trenches, and now people meant to put a stop to it.

From Princess E. Bluecher, *An English Wife in Berlin*, Constable, 1920.

Questions

1 What reasons does the Kaiser give for leaving for Holland?

2 What impression is he trying to give of his behaviour?

3 What does the cartoon imply are the Kaiser's reasons for going to Holland?

4 Does Princess Bluecher's description of the scenes in Berlin support the Kaiser's view of his troops as 'still faithful'?

5 What might have been the mood of the crowds if Wilhelm's abdication had not een announced?

6 What word or phrase conveys Princess Bluecher's own attitude towards the crowds?

7 Imagine you join the huge crowds in Berlin's streets and talk to others. Some are supporters of revolution, some want the Kaiser to stay, some are confused. Make notes on your conversations.

8 It is dawn and bitterly cold on the morning of 10 November 1918. The Kaiser and a group of officers are waiting at the Dutch border Describe the thoughts that might have been going through Wilhelm's mind.

3 Germany becomes a republic

On the afternoon of 9 November Prince Max handed over as Chancellor to Fritz Ebert, the leader of the German socialists. Shortly afterwards, the socialists set up a republic in place of Wilhelm's empire and Ebert became its first president. On 11 November his new government signed an armistice with the Allies to end the war. Germany's misery did not end, however, because the Allies went on with their sea blockade, which stopped food and other vital supplies reaching Germany.

Ebert's government was blamed for all Germany's difficulties: for defeat, the food shortages, and the disorder in the towns where bands of workers and soldiers were taking the law into their own hands. It was also under attack from other political groups. To the right were all those who had been opposed to the overthrow of the emperor. To them Ebert was a traitor to his country. On the left were extreme socialist groups, who often had links with the Communists who had just taken power in Russia. To them, Ebert was a class traitor who enjoyed power and wearing top hat and tails, the uniform of a middle-class politician, even though he was an ex-saddle maker.

Princess Bluecher's diary (Source A) gives some idea of the chaos and hardship in the early days of the Republic. In the last section she makes a criticism of Ebert. In Source B the Communist paper, the Red Stick, *puts it in a different way.*

A Princess Bluecher's diary

1 *The Armistice* (12 November)

The few people I have already spoken to were desperate and horrified at the terms of the armistice, especially that the blockade is not to be raised, which means for so many people a gradual death from exhaustion. . . . A diet of heavy vegetables cooked without fat of any kind, with dry bread and potatoes is not in the long run consistent with the nerve power necessary under the circumstances.

From Princess E. Bluecher, *An English Wife in Berlin*, Constable, 1920.

2 *Shortages* (December)

For years people have been struggling along, supporting as best they could the absence of everything conducive to decent existence, but now it is almost impossible to bear it any longer. The ancient boots and shoes defy any more mending, the stockings consist of a series of patches, dresses and mantles have been turned and dyed year after year, and most people's underwear has no recognisable resemblance to the dainty garments of pre-war times. . . . As there is no soap, our linen issues from the wash-tub greyer and more hopelessly torn than we ever dared imagine and certainly the German woman of today is the worst-clad of all Europe.

3 *Lawlessness* (December)

In Berlin the soldiers and workmen are disturbing all the existing law and order, dismissing the local boards* without creating any new ones to take their place. Armed deserters and rowdies force the authorities to resign office at the point of their bayonets. Public and private food

* local government organisations

supplies are plundered and confiscated by bands of individuals, who terrorize over the unarmed civilians. Strikes are weakening and endangering the little life that is left ... millions of people out of work, yet everything is at stagnation point. Daily the traffic is stopped by the demonstrations and counter-demonstrations which are the order of the day ... the results are street frays like the one on the evening of December 6th, when 14 innocent men and women were killed.

4 *The Government* (December)

The socialists have not had time to develop a really strong government, or to test the practical working of theories in a country which is still at heart for the greater part monarchical in its sympathies.

I believe that the German people in reality need something for their imagination – a figurehead that represents in some way the fantastic, the unusual, the ideal. There is no poetry in the figure of a short, stout President with a bald head, a top-hat and a black coat.

B A Communist view of Ebert

'*Germany, you have a pig of a problem*'.

Cartoon by George Grosz (undated), Imperial War Museum, Freikorps Exhibition, 1984.

Questions

1 What is a blockade?

2 What would be the effect on German families of having to live on the diet Princess Bluecher describes?

3 Why were people finding it *especially* hard to put up with the shortages by the end of 1918?

4 What can you find in Princess Bluecher's entries to (a) support and (b) contradict the view that Ebert's government was unable to control the situation?

5 What might the demonstrations and counter-demonstrations have been about?

6 Why were the streets of Berlin particularly dangerous for someone like Princess Bluecher in the months after the revolution?

7 Do her descriptions give any clues as to where her sympathies lie?

8 What does 'monarchical' mean? Do you think it likely that Princess Bluecher was a monarchist?

9 What is the Princess's view of Ebert as head of the German nation?

10 In which way does the *Red Stick* cartoon give the same *information* as Princess Bluecher? Explain how it gives a different *interpretation*.

4 The Republic under attack

In the spring of 1919 Berlin and most of Germany was in chaos with daily strikes, demonstrations, street fights and political murders. In desperation President Ebert turned for help to the army. It was eager to crush left-wing groups such as the Spartacists who founded the German Communist Party in January 1919. They took the lead in organising a rising in Berlin when most public buildings were taken over by armed groups of workers. Richard Watt, an historian writing in 1968, reconstructed the army's brutal killing of the two main Spartacist leaders, Rosa Luxemburg and Karl Liebknecht (Source A). As well as the regular army, there were Freikorps *troops involved.*

The Freikorps *were volunteer bands of ex-soldiers recruited with Ebert's agreement to help deal with the disorders. It was embarrassing for the socialist government that the* Freikorps *were responsible for some of the most savage attacks on working-class and trade union organisations. Source B is a recruiting poster for the* Freikorps *which suggests some reasons why they appealed to the German people, especially at a time when Poland was ready to take over some of the eastern lands of defeated Germany.*

The threats to the government and to law and order were just as strong from the right as from the left. In 1922 two right-wing nationalists assassinated the foreign minister, Walter Rathenau. He was an object of hate to the nationalists because he was willing to talk to leaders of the countries who had defeated Germany – and because he was a Jew. Source C is part of the tribute to Walter Rathenau given in the Reichstag, or parliament, by Chancellor Wirth.

A Murder of the Spartacists

At 9 pm on January 15 a patrol from the Horse Guards Division broke into the apartment and seized the three Communist leaders, who apparently had been betrayed by a neighbour. . . . They were taken to headquarters in the Eden Hotel for questioning, in the course of which they were beaten. Later in the night, automobiles were brought round to the back entrance of the hotel, and Liebknecht and Luxemburg were brought out separately. As Liebknecht emerged through the doorway, a *Freikorps* soldier, an enormously built private named Runge, raised his rifle and smashed it down on Liebknecht's head. More dead than alive, 'Spartakus' was flung into a car. Six *Freikorps* officers climbed in, and the automobile drove off towards Moabit prison.

A few moments later Rosa Luxemburg hobbled out through the same hotel doorway. She too was clubbed with Runge's rifle. She too, almost lifeless, was thrown into an automobile, which drove off under the command of a Lieutenant Vogel. Meanwhile the car bearing Liebknecht had stopped in the wooded Tiergarten, a few blocks north of the hotel. Leibknecht was taken out of the car by the six officers, who later claimed that the vehicle had broken down. He was asked if he

From R. M. Watt, *The Kings Depart*, Weidenfeld and Nicolson, 1968.

could walk and replied that he could. According to the *Freikorps* officers he broke loose and was shot twice while 'attempting to escape'.

No one knows whether Rosa Luxemburg was still alive when Lieutenant Vogel blew out her brains with a single shot. Her automobile was stopped and the body was thrown off the Liechtenstein Bridge into the ice-covered Landswehr Canal from which it was not recovered until May 31.

B   Recruiting for the Freikorps

'Comrade! help me! against Bolshevism, the Polish threat, and famine.'

C Responsibility for Rathenau's murder

I was witness of important discussions of our murdered friend with the most powerful of the Allied statesmen in Genoa. You could not have found a more eloquent advocate in small, intimate discussions – serious discussions – than Dr Rathenau.... But what were his motives according to the right-wing press? Indeed what I read ... that all the treaties are concluded only so that he can enrich himself and his Jewish relatives, then you will understand that our German fatherland is being driven irrevocably to ruin by the rabble-rouser.... Every mouth must speak to do away with this atmosphere of murder, of quarrel, of poison! There is the enemy who injects his poison into the wounds of the people. There is the enemy – and there is no doubt about it: this enemy is on the right.

From A. Brecht, *The Political Education of Arnold Brecht*, Princeton University Press, 1970.

Questions

1 Which of the sources is a secondary source? In what ways might it be (a) more reliable and (b) less reliable than a primary source for the same event?

2 What evidence is there in Source A that the army and *Freikorps* were operating in a lawless way?

3 What does Source A tell you about the difficulties faced by Ebert's government?

4 In Source B what do you think is represented by the eagle and the man in uniform?

5 What evidence does Source B give for reasons why many Germans looked on the *Freikorps* as a heroic group of men?

6 Chancellor Wirth in Source C attacks the right wing. What do you understand by the right and left in German politics at this time?

7 What is anti-semitism? What evidence is there in Wirth's speech that the right wing was anti-semitic?

8 What possible reasons could the right have had for spreading anti-semitic stories?

9 Discuss whether Ebert's use of violent men to defend the Republic in 1919 paved the way for events such as the murder of Rathenau in 1922.

5 The shock of Versailles

When news of the peace terms under discussion at Versailles leaked out German newspapers proclaimed, 'Shame', 'Enslavement', 'The Fatherland has been cheated'. Much of the shock came from the feeling that President Wilson had broken his promise that Germany would not be treated as a conquered nation now she had got rid of her emperor and military government. Princess Bluecher's diary for February 1919 describes these reactions in Source A. The mood in Britain and France is portrayed in a Punch cartoon (Source C) and a remark (Source D) made by the French President, Georges Clemenceau, when the terms of the peace treaty were published in May. The German Chancellor, Philip Scheidemann, resigned rather than sign and he defended this action in his autobiography written in the 1920 (Source B). Toni Sender, a young Frankfurt editor, believed Germany had to sign, as she explains in her autobiography written in the 1930s (Source E).

A Reactions in Germany

I have listened to the voices of every class of people here, and I sometimes fear that England has missed the right moment for restoring touch with the German people, and laying the foundation for a lasting peace in Europe. After the revolution, in the great wave of reaction against the war which set in here, the Entente could have done anything with the German people had they made the slightest overture towards reconciliation. People were ready here to make reparation for the wrong done by their leaders. But now they say that Wilson has broken his word, and an undying hatred will be smouldering in the heart of every German. Over and over again I hear the same refrain, 'We shall hate our conquerors with a hatred that will only cease when the day of our revenge comes again.'

From Princess E. Bluecher, *An English Wife in Berlin*, Constable, 1920.

B The German Chancellor resigns

The Peace Treaty handed to these delegates on 7th May was the most iniquitous piece of work ever produced by blind hatred and senseless fury. Prince Max's Government, in its telegraphic communications with Wilson, took expressly as its basis the points formulated by the President of the USA . . . solemn assurances that 'the Entente was not waging war against the German people, but against Kaiserism and Prussian militarism'. Although the Kaiser had fled and was therefore non-existent, although Prussian militarism lay prostrate on the ground, while the countries of the Entente were armed to the teeth, although a Parliament elected by the people and a government with a Social Democratic President and Premier represented the German nation – in spite of all this, here was this mad, dictated Treaty, by which a people of seventy millions was to be enslaved and shorn of its honour and defence for scores of years. . . . What hand would not wither that binds itself and us in these fetters?

From P. Scheidemann, *Memoirs of a Social Democrat* (trans. J. E. Michell), Hodder and Stoughton, 1929.

From *Punch*, 19 February 1919.

GIVING HIM ROPE?

GERMAN CRIMINAL (*to Allied Police*). "HERE, I SAY, STOP! YOU'RE HURTING ME! [*Aside*] IF I ONLY WHINE ENOUGH I MAY BE ABLE TO WRIGGLE OUT OF THIS YET."

D The French President's view

'Eat, bird or die – sign you Boches, or we'll advance.'

From P. Scheidemann, *Memoirs of a Social Democrat* (trans. J. E. Michell), Hodder and Stoughton, 1929.

E Why Germany should sign

What should we do? ... What was the alternative of not signing? Impossible to call the people of Germany to arms for new resistance! The German people definitely wanted peace, were exhausted. Not to sign would mean occupation of the most important territories containing raw materials, intensification of the blockade, unemployment, hunger, the death of thousands, the holding back of our war prisoners – a catastrophe which finally would force us to sign still more humiliating conditions. . . . I finally decided to advocate signing.

From Toni Sender, *The Autobiography of a German Rebel*, Routledge, 1940.

Questions

1 What does Princess Bluecher mean by 'the Entente'? What mistake does she think it was making over the peace terms?

2 What would have been the feelings of most Germans if they had seen the *Punch* cartoon?

3 What does President Clemenceau's remark tell you about his attitude to Germany? Was this a statesmanlike comment? Explain your answer.

4 What is Philip Scheidemann's case for believing that the Germans had won the right to be treated as equals in the peace treaty?

5 Which of the points made by Scheidemann agrees with a statement in Princess Bluecher's diary?

6 What did Scheidemann mean by writing of a 'dictated Treaty'?

7 In Source E Toni Sender describes why she decided her newspaper would support signing the treaty. Use her reasons to write an article which might have appeared in the paper.

6 Occupation of the Ruhr

The Allies decided that Germany should pay nearly £6600 million in reparations for war damages. This was an enormous sum when the German economy was in ruins from the war and the blockade and when the Versailles Treaty had taken away vital industrial regions. Because of this the Allies allowed Germany a moratorium (or delay) in payment in 1921. But when she failed to come up with some payments at the end of 1922 the French President, Raymiond Poincaré, was convinced that Germany was deliberately getting into economic difficulties.. On 11 January 1923 he ordered French troops, supported by Belgians, to occupy the Ruhr, Germany's main coal and steel area. The people of the Ruhr refused to co-operate with the invaders and the main unions went on strike. The German government supported them and made up for the loss of production by printing money which led to the inflation described in Unit 7.

Life in the occupied zone is remembered by an SA officer (see page 42) who was a boy at the time (Source A) and is described in German government reports (Source B). The British government disagreed with the occupation policy. One of its reasons is illustrated in the cartoon (Source C), and the British ambassador in Berlin showed in his diary (Source D) how he thought the Germans had even gained something from the occupation.

A Living under occupation

Then came the news that Wiesbaden, our own lovely resort city, would fall in the occupied zone. We received appropriate rules of conduct at school; but we all knew that none of us would ever salute a French officer. Better hide behind a strange doorway than doff our caps to the enemy.

The advance guard of the French arrived. And if we had no direct knowledge of misery in war time, we did then. Traffic was at a standstill, food became scarce, and the conduct of the army of occupation was in no wise conciliatory. . . . No one travelled on the state railway, run by the French with the assistance of several Germans whom we considered traitors. It would have been as good as taking one's life in one's hands, since no one knew when a train would be derailed. In any case, to patronize the railway would have been treason in our eyes; rather suffer discomforts for hours enthroned on barrels high up on freight trucks – but travel by train – never!

From Theodore Abel, *Why Hitler came to Power*, Prentice Hall, 1938.

B Government Report on the occupied zone

March 13th 1923
In the neighbourhood of Essen, Josephine Mlaker was violated by six French soldiers. At Langendreer (Ruhr) the railway offices have been looted. At Buer (Ruhr) two security police officials were summarily shot.

From the London School of Economics Archives: German Embassy Press Information, Government Reports.

March 17th 1923

At Dortmund French soldiers forcibly entered shops and requisitioned large quantities of furniture and other household goods. At Orsey, near Duesseldorf, the Belgians seized funds intended for Ruhr-relief. At Muenchen-Gladbach, near Cologne, the French seized 68,000,000 paper marks at the Reichsbank Branch. At Juelich, near Dusseldorf, the French entered the Savings Bank and seized funds intended for Ruhr-relief.

A British and French disagreement

From *Punch*, 10 January 1923.

THE GOOSE THAT COULDN'T—OR WOULDN'T.

Mr. Bonar Law. "THE WRETCHED BIRD CAN'T LAY GOLDEN EGGS WITHOUT A NICE LONG MORATORIUM."

M. Poincaré. "AND I SAY SHE CAN. AND A GOOSE THAT CAN LAY AND WON'T LAY MUST BE MADE TO LAY—EVEN IF I HAVE TO WRING HER NECK!"

D The British ambassador's assessment

The French, by their invasion of the Ruhr, and by their imprisonment of mine directors have done more to bring together all parties and all classes in Germany than it was possible to effect by any other means. The mine-owners and mine-directors who have been imprisoned are becoming national heroes. They do not deserve to be. . . . They have ruined large classes of their countrymen by their inflation policy, and without doing much good to themselves; but they have achieved the object dearest to their heart, which was to avoid the payment of reparation to France. For the moment, all class hostility of the workmen against the owners has been submerged by the patriotic wave. The whole country appears to be united.

From Lord D'Aberon, *Ambassador of Peace*, Hodder and Stoughton, 1929.

Questions

1 What evidence is there in Source A about the extent of the Ruhr people's dislike of the occupation?

2 Give two reasons why the boy never travelled by train at this time.

3 How does the government report support or contradict the comment in Source A that the occupation was 'in no wise conciliatory'?

4 Suggest reasons why the German government had this report written and what they hoped to do with it. How does your answer affect the report's value as evidence?

5 Which leader is portrayed most sympathetically in the cartoon?

6 How does the cartoonist see the different views of France and Britain about forcing Germany to pay reparations?

7 Use the ambassador's diary to list ways in which he believed the Germans were (a) gaining and (b) losing from the occupation.

7 Germany's 'maddest year'

At the beginning of January 1923, one German mark was worth about 10.5 dollars; by the end of the month it took 43,000 marks to buy a dollar. The 'great inflation' had begun. Germany's economy had been in difficulties since the war, and confidence in the value of her currency collapsed when she failed to make her reparation payments and the Ruhr was occupied. The goverment's policy of printing more paper money meant that the mark lost all value.

Source A comes from the 1941 autobiography of a German who was a student in 1923 and Source B is a letter from a young Englishwoman. The cartoonist in Source C is commenting that the USSR's rouble already had no real value in the rest of the world and the French were nervous about the effect of the mark's collapse on the franc. Source D describes the problems for banks.

A Living with inflation: the student's view

Billion-mark bank notes were quickly handed on as though they burned one's fingers, for tomorrow one would no longer pay in notes but in bushels of notes.

From Eitel Wolf Dobert, *Convert to Freedom* (trans. Heinz and Ruth Norden), John Lane/Bodley Head, 1941.

Inflation – that meant that an uncle sent us money specifically intended on the money order for a new pair of shoes. By the time the mail clerk had paid out the amount, it was barely sufficient for a pair of socks; and by afternoon, when the gates opened for the customary two hours of leave, the purchasing power of the money had declined to the level of a pair of shoe-laces. . . .

One afternoon I rang Aunt Louise's bell. The door was opened merely a crack. From the dark came an old, broken voice. 'Oh, it's you, son! Just think, I've used 60 billion marks worth of gas. My milk bill is one billion. But all I have left is two thousand marks! I don't understand it any more, I don't understand it. . . .'

'But why don't you let me in, Aunt?' I pushed the door open. She must be living on another planet. I really should have to enlighten her!

When I departed after hours trying to explain to her how many millions there were in a billion and how many billions in a trillion, she pressed an envelope into my hand.

'Open it outside, it's a little surprise for you! Go on – don't thank me!'

Outside, in the light of a street lamp, I opened the envelope. It contained a crisp new twenty mark note. Thoughtfully I tore it up.

B An English girl writes home: 1923, Frankfurt am Main

Dear Father,

As I told you, I am appalled every week when I see the names of
the people who are now obliged to receive support from the Welfare:
teachers, elderly nurses, artists, musicians, journalists. They receive the
princely sum of 3,000 marks a month. The town can't do more, and
is really doing all that is possible, but when margarine costs 3,600
marks a lb and a loaf of bread 720 marks – well you can think the rest
out for yourself. Even people earning good incomes cannot make both
ends meet; the old people are in a worse plight still; they have no firing,
no shoes, no linen. . . . If only foreigners would not judge Germany by
the restaurants and theatres.'

From the London
School of Economics
Archives: German
Embassy Press
Information.

C International repercussions

From *Punch*, 15
August 1923.

THE EXCHANGE ASYLUM.

Rouble. "WHAT'S YOUR NAME?"
Mark. "MARK."
Rouble. "WHAT ARE YOU DOING?"
Mark. "FALLING."
Rouble. "WHAT'S YOUR FACE VALUE?"
Mark. "A SHILLING."
Rouble. "WHAT ARE YOU WORTH NOW?"
Mark. "TWENTY MILLION TO THE POUND."
Rouble. "COME INSIDE."
Franc (*nervously*). "I'M NOT FEELING TOO SANE MYSELF."

D   A standard bank letter: 1923

The bank deeply regrets that it can no longer administer your deposit of 68,000 marks, since the costs are out of all proportion to the capital. We are therefore taking the liberty of returning your capital. Since we have no bank-notes in small enough denominations at our disposal, we have rounded out the sum to one million marks.

A cancelled stamp for 5,000,000 marks adorned the envelope.

From Konrad Heiden, *Der Fuehrer* (trans. Ralph Manhelm), Houghton Mifflin, 1944.

Questions

1 Choose the example from all the sources which you think explains the effect of the German inflation in the most memorable way.

2 From Sources A and B, which group of German people suffered most from the inflation?

3 What thoughts might have gone through the student's mind as he tore up his aunt's gift?

4 Explain why the bank needed to write a standard letter to customers such as the one in Source D?

5 What kind of person might have received such a letter? How would the person feel on reading it? How do you think the great inflation has affected the person's life?

6 Why do you think the girl in Source B felt the need to explain the difficulties of the German people to her father in so much detail?

7 In January 1923 the pound was divided into twenty shillings (5p). Use the cartoon to explain what inflation meant to the exchange value of the mark.

8 Does the evidence in the other sources support the cartoonist's view that the inflation was a form of insanity?

Part 2

The Nazis and Weimar

8 Hitler enters politics

Corporal Hitler had been twice wounded and twice honoured but in 1918 he had no home, family, or trade. The army selected him for the job of trying to draw soldiers away from revolutionary or socialist ideas. In September 1919 Hitler was sent to investigate the German Workers' Party in Munich. Its members did not talk about a government take-over of industry or farms and felt no solidarity with workers in other countries, but they were passionate about making Germany powerful again. Hitler joined them. Within a year he had become the Party's propaganda chief and encouraged it to take a new name, the National Socialist German Workers' Party (NSDAP). The selection from its 26-point programme in Source A shows how the party set out to appeal to both right and left.

In October 1920 a secret policeman in the German state of Bavaria was sent to listen to Hitler speaking in a Munich beer cellar. His report (Source B) shows which parts of the programme Hitler stressed most in those early years.

A Programme of the National Socialist German Workers' Party: 24 February 1920

1 We demand the Union of all Germans in a Greater Germany on the basis of the right of national self-determination.

2 We demand equality of rights for the German people in its dealings with other nations and the revocation* of the peace treaties of Versailles and Saint Germain.

3 We demand land and territory (colonies) to feed our people and to settle our surplus population.

4 Only members of the nation may be citizens of the state. Only those of German blood, whatever their creed, may be members of the nation. Accordingly, no Jew may be a member of the nation.

5 Non-citizens may live in Germany only as guests . . .

9 All citizens shall have equal rights and duties.

11 We demand the nationalization of all businesses which have been formed into corporations (trusts).

14 We demand profit-sharing in large industrial enterprises.

15 We demand extensive development of insurance for old age.

16 We demand the creation and maintenance of a healthy middle class, the immediate communalizing of big department stores, and their lease at a cheap rate to small traders.

From J. Noakes and G. Pridham, *Documents on Nazism*, Jonathan Cape, 1974.

* cancellation

B Hitler speaks in Munich, October 1920

We need some national pride again. But who can the nation be proud of these days? Of Ebert? (laughter) Of the Government? We need a national will just as much. We must not always say: 'We can't do that.' We must be able to do it. In order to smash this disgraceful peace treaty, we must regard every means as justified. (loud applause) First, there must be a nationalist mood and then will come the economic prosperity of the nation. We must have blind faith in our future . . . .

Now Hitler turned to deal with the Right and the Left. The Nationalists on the Right lack a social sense, the Socialists on the Left a nationalist one. He appeals to the parties on the Right: If you want to be nationalists then come down among your people and put away all your class pride. To the Left he appeals: You who proclaim your solidarity with the whole world, first show your solidarity with your own compatriots, be Germans first and foremost.

Then Hitler turned to the future of Germany, to the youth of Germany, and in particular, with warm words for their intellectual leaders, the German students. Your place is with us, with the people. You are still young and still have the fire of enthusiasm in your veins, come over to us, join our fighting party, which pursues its aims ruthlessly, with every means, even with force! (loud applause) We are not a class party, but the party of honest workers . . . .

From J. Noakes and G. Pridham, *Documents on Nazism*, Jonathan Cape, 1974.

Questions

1 Make a table with four headings: most German men and women; extreme nationalists; trade unionists and socialists; the middle classes. Under each heading put the number of any programme point which would appeal to them. What does your table show about the political skill of the leaders who wrote the programme?

2 From Source A explain what is meant by 'the right of national self-determination'. In 1920 which Germans felt they had lost this right?

3 Which German-speaking people were most affected by the Treaty of Saint Germain?

4 What evidence of anti-semitism can you find in this programme?

5 Why did the audience in Source B laugh at the mention of Ebert? What does this tell you about the kind of people in the audience?

6 How did Hitler try to make his party attractive to the young?

7 Explain what Hitler meant when he said the right lacked a 'social sense' and the left a 'nationalist' one.

8 Why do you think the authorities sent a secret policeman to this meeting?

9 Hitler: the public figure

In June 1921 the NSDAP made Adolf Hitler its chairman and leader. He soon became well known as a powerful public speaker who could win over huge audiences and hold them spellbound.

Kurt Ludecke, Ernst Hanfstaengl and Dr Karl von Mueller all heard Hitler speak for the first time in the early 1920s. Ludecke (Source A) was a supporter and fund raiser for the Nazi Party throughout the twenties, but when Hitler came to power he had him locked up in Dachau concentration camp. From there Ludecke escaped to the United States where he wrote his autobiography in the late 1930s.

Ernst Hanfstaengl (Source B) befriended Hitler in 1921 and introduced him to Munich society. He later rose to become the foreign press chief for the party, but fell out with Hitler and had to flee from Germany in 1937. He too went to America, but it wasn't until much later in 1957 that he published his recollections of Hitler.

Dr Mueller, a Professor of History in Munich who later gave evidence at Hitler's trial in 1923, was present at the first NSDAP rally. His memoirs (Source C) give us an idea of how professionally the party staged their rallies.

A   Hitler speaks: August 1922

An excited, expectant crowd was now filling the beautiful square to the last inch and overflowing into surrounding streets. There were well over a hundred thousand .... I was close enough to see Hitler's face, watch every change in his expression, hear every word he said.

When the man stepped forward on the platform, there was no applause. He stood silent for a moment. Then be began to speak, quietly and ingratiating at first. Before long his voice had risen to a hoarse shriek that gave an extraordinary effect of an intensity of feeling ....

Critically, I studied this slight, pale man, his brown hair parted on one side and falling again and again over his sweating brow, threatening and beseeching, with small, pleading hands and flashing, steel-blue eyes, he had the look of a fanatic.

Presently, my critical faculty was swept away. Leaning from the tribune as if he were trying to impel his inner self into the consciousness of all these thousands, he was holding the masses, and me with them, under a hypnotic spell by the sheer force of his conviction ....

I do not know how to describe the emotions that swept over me as I heard this man. His words were like a scourge. When he spoke of the disgrace of Germany, I felt ready to spring on any enemy.... I forgot everything but the man; then, glancing round, I saw that his magnetism was holding these thousands as one!

From Kurt Ludecke, *I knew Hitler*, Charles Scribner's Sons, 1937.

B Hitler speaks: November 1922

I looked round at the audience. Where was the nondescript crowd I had seen only an hour before? What was suddenly holding these people, who, on the hopeless incline of the falling mark, were engaged in a daily struggle to keep themselves within the line of decency? The hubbub and mug-clattering had stopped and they were drinking in every word. Only a few yards away was a young woman, her eyes fastened on the speaker. Transfixed as though in some devotional ecstacy, she had ceased to be herself and was completely under the spell of Hitler's despotic faith in Germany's future greatness.

From Ernst Hanfstaengl, *Hitler: The Missing Years*, Eyre and Spottiswoode, 1957.

C The Nazis' first rally: Munich 1923

On the 28th January 6,000 SA men lined up on the Marsfeld .... 'Their own battle songs, their own flags, their own symbols, their own salute.' I noted down, 'military-like stewards, a forest of bright red flags with black swastika on white ground, a mixture of the military and the revolutionary, of nationalist and socialist. . . . For hours endless booming military music; for hours, short speeches by subordinate leaders. When was he coming? Had something unexpected happened? Nobody can describe the fever that spread in this atmosphere. Suddenly, there was a movement at the back entrance. Words of command. The speaker on the platform stopped in mid-sentence. Everybody jumped up saluting. And right through the shouting crowds and the streaming flags the one they were all waiting for came.

From J. Noakes and G. Pridham, *Documents on Nazism*, Jonathan Cape, 1974.

Questions

1 What effect did Hitler have on Kurt Ludecke personally when he heard him for the first time (Source A)?

2 Can you find any explanation in Ludecke's account for Hitler's 'magnetism' over the rest of the audience?

3 Does the Ernst Hanfstaengl report (Source B) support or contradict Ludecke's?

4 What did Hanfstaengl mean by 'the hopeless incline of the mark'?

5 Think of someone today who is successful at capturing the attention of large crowds. Analyse how it is done and compare his/her methods with Hitler's.

6 How does Dr Mueller's account (Source C) suggest different reasons for Hitler's power over crowds from the other two accounts?

7 Which of these accounts is likely to be most reliable? Give your reasons.

8 Do you think you would have been impressed by Hitler if you had been at one of these rallies? Why?

10 Hitler: the private individual

As Hitler built up his personal following in the early 1920s he was introduced to wealthy families in Munich's smart society. They liked to invite him to parties in their drawing rooms, or salons, because he was something of a curiosity with his Charlie Chaplin-like appearance and awkward manner. Some were amused at the difference between his awkward shyness in private and his self-confidence in public.

Hitler never really gave up the rough and ready habits of his pre-war days as a down-and-out in Vienna. He avoided regular hours and regular work whenever he could, much to the fury of his party colleagues. One of them, Kurt Ludecke, was Hitler's political adviser in these early years in Munich. Source A is taken from his autobiography, written after he had fled to the United States in the 1930s. He recalls how Hitler was first introduced to polite society by 'Putzi' (Ernst) Hanfstaengl, a wealthy publisher. Source B is set in the 1930s after Hitler came to power. Albert Speer, then Hitler's favourite architect and later his Minister of War Production, recalls a typical evening in the Chancellor's official residence in Berlin. The extract is from Speer's memoirs, mostly written while he was serving twenty years for war crimes.

A Hitler enters Munich society

Putzi's comfortable and cultivated home was unquestionably the first house of the kind to open its doors to Hitler. He seemed to feel at ease with Hanfstaengl's pretty wife and handsome children. Putzi played Wagner beautifully, and Hitler, who loved music, ranked Wagner among the demi-gods.

From Kurt Ludecke, *I knew Hitler*, Charles Scribner's Sons, 1937.

In time Hanfstaengl made himself a sort of social-secretary to Hitler, zealous in introducing him to hostesses. Hitler still had an air of shyness in the presence of those who had wealth or social authority. But his very naivety in social matters tempted the salons to lionize him. He was asked many places, and was received always with delight, though sometimes with amusement.

For instance, Putzi introduced him to the Bruckmanns, who had a fine house with good pictures and books, tasteful furniture, and excellent food. I can still see Frau Bruckmann's eyes shining as she described Hitler's truly touching dismay before an artichoke.

'But madam,' he had said in his softest voice, 'you must tell me how to eat this thing. I never saw one before.'

In those days his naivety was sincere and genuine.

Indeed, it was a little too genuine. Hitler loved beauty and appreciated good taste, but it never occurred to him to consider himself as an object that people might examine with curious eyes. I soon gave up my futile efforts to induce him to give more heed to his person and dress, though it might have been advantageous for the leader of the Party to appear less like a refugee. He clung to his shapeless trench-coat and clumsy shoes. His hair still fell over his eyes at every vehement gesture during his speeches. He continued to eat in a hurry, some messy stuff or other, while he ran from place to place. If you succeeded in making him stand still long enough to confer on important matters, he would take out of his pocket a piece of greasy sausage and a slice of bread, and bolt them while he talked. The only improvement I was able to persuade him to, was to give up his ugly and uncomfortable hard collars for more suitable soft ones. He would never resent my suggestions, but simply ignore them.

B Dreary nights in the Chancellery

From six to eight persons would assemble on those evenings: his adjutants, his doctor, the photographer Hoffmann, one or two Munich acquaintances, quite often Hitler's pilot Bauer along with his radio man. . . . This was the most private circle in Berlin for political associates such as Goebbels were usually not wanted in the evenings. . . . The talk wandered off into trivialities. Hitler liked to hear about the theatre. Scandals also interested him. The pilot talked about flying . . . . But usually Hitler would tell stories about his life and development.

From Albert Speer, *Inside the Third Reich*, Sphere, 1975.

Kannenburg, the house steward, did try a few times to serve better food for these rather private meals. For a few weeks Hitler actually ate caviar by the spoonful with gusto, and praised the taste, which was new to him. But then he asked Kannenburg about the price, was horrified, and gave strict orders against ever having that again. . . .

After supper the company moved into the salon. . . . Everyone settled into easy chairs; Hitler unbuttoned his jacket and stretched out his legs. The lights slowly dimmed . . . The first movie began. There we sat . . . for some three or four hours, and when these films came to an end at about one in the morning, we stood up stiff and dazed.

Questions

1 Does Kurt Ludecke's account give evidence that Hitler was completely embarrassed in cultivated homes? What other reasons might Hitler have had for behaving in this way?

2 Have you ever found yourself in a similar situation to the one at the Bruckmann dinner party? Describe what happened.

3 In which ways did Kurt Ludecke think Hitler might be a drawback for the Nazi Party?

4 With which groups, and for what reasons, might Hitler's appearance have been an advantage?

5 Many accounts of Hitler's social life agree with Speer's (Source B). How do you think that a person who spent most evenings in this way could hold such power?

11 The Hitler Putsch, November 1923

By November 1923 the Weimar government was thoroughly unpopular for not controlling inflation. In Bavaria, Hitler and General von Ludendorff, a First World War hero, saw a chance to overthrow the Bavarian government in Munich. Their rising or 'Putsch' began in a beer cellar where the Bavarian governor, von Kahr, was making a speech. Von Kahr may have been in league with the plotters for he was freed after Hitler took over the beer cellar with the help of Hermann Goering and 'brownshirts' of the Nazi private army. However, von Kahr then sent a warning to Berlin. As a result the 'victory' parade the next day was broken up by armed police and the Reichswehr, the German army.

Ernst Hanfstaengl was with Hitler in the beer cellar. In his autobiography (Source A), written in the 1950s, he describes what happened. Professor von Mueller was in the audience and gave evidence (Source B) at Hitler's trial.

The march through Munich is described (Source C) by Kurt Ludecke in his autobiography, using descriptions given to him by the leading National Socialists who took part. Ludecke was an adviser to Hitler at the time. The second description (Source D) is from the report of an inquiry into the Putsch.

A A supporter in the beer cellar

Kahr was on his feet, droning away at some boring speech. I said to myself, 'This waiting is dull enough, but there's no need to go thirsty.' So I went over to the serving hatch and got three litre jugs of beer. I remember they cost a billion marks a piece . . .

. . . the door behind us flew open and in burst Goering . . . plus about twenty-five brownshirts with pistols and machine guns. What an uproar. Everything happened at once, Hitler began to plough his way towards the platform and the rest of us surged behind him. Tables overturned with their jugs of beer . . . Hitler clambered on to a chair and fired a round at the ceiling . . . 'The national revolution has broken out. The Reichswehr is with us. Our flag is flying on their barracks.'

From Ernst Hanfstaengl, Hitler: The Missing Years, Eyre and Spottiswoode, 1957.

B A witness of the Putsch

. . . the general mood – I can of course only judge from my surroundings, but I think that this represented the general feeling in the hall – was still against the whole business. . . . The change came only during Hitler's second speech when he entered about ten minutes later, went to the platform and made a short speech. In a few sentences it totally transformed the mood of the audience. I have rarely experienced anything like it. When he stepped on to the platform the disturbance was so great that he could not be heard, and he fired a shot. I can still see the gesture. . . . When things did not become quiet, he shouted angrily at the audience: 'If you are not quiet, I shall have a machine gun put up on the gallery.'

From J. Noakes and G. Pridham, Documents on Nazism, Jonathan Cape, 1974.

C The 'victory march': a Nazi view

In the hour before noon about 7,000 men, in files eight abreast, marched over the Iskar bridge into the inner city followed by thousands of Nazis and their sympathisers. Ahead was the Ludwig Strasse* blocked by the Reichswehr. The flood advanced. In its front rank marched Hitler, Ludendorff and other leaders . . . steadily they went on in the face of the waiting troops . . . .

A cold-blooded officer ordered his platoon to fire on the Nazis. He repeated the order twice, then tore a rifle from the hands of a reluctant soldier. Streicher screamed: 'Ludendorff – don't shoot your General!' It was too late. A volley rent the air killing 14 men in the Nazi ranks. Ludendorff, erect and unhurt, marched straight ahead and was arrested. Hitler, who had been at Ludendorff's side, was dragged to the ground with a dislocated shoulder . . . .

. . . the crowds in the rear wavered and halted. The panic seized the street. In a desperate scramble for safety everyone fled.

From Kurt Ludecke, *I knew Hitler*, Charles Scribner's Sons, 1937.

* *street*

D The 'victory march': an official view

The column of National Socialists 2,000 strong, nearly all armed, moved on through the Zweibruecken Strasse. . . . Ceaseless shouts of 'Stop! Don't go on!' by the state police were not obeyed . . . . Police officers were spat upon, and pistols with the safety catches off were stuck in their chests. The police used rubber truncheons and rifle butts and tried to push back the crowd. . . . Suddenly, a National Socialist fired a pistol at a police officer from close quarters . . . a shot gun battle ensued. . . . After no more than 30 seconds the Hitler lot fled.

From J. Noakes and G. Pridham, *Documents on Nazism*, Jonathan Cape, 1974.

Questions

1 How can you tell from Source A that the Putsch took place at the height of the inflation?

2 Why do you think Hitler claimed that 'The Reichswehr are with us'?

3 From Sources A and B do you think that taking control of the beer cellar was real proof of National Socialist strength?

4 Which aspects of Hanfstaengl's account are confirmed in von Mueller's evidence?

5 In source C, what did the Nazi leader Streicher intend when he screamed, 'Ludendorff – don't shoot your General'?

6 List the points of disagreement in the two descriptions of the march.

7 Who does (a) Kurt Ludecke, (b) the official report blame for the shooting?

8 Take Sources C and D in turn and explain what bias the authors show.

12 For and against the Putsch

The Hitler Putsch failed. Its leaders were arrested and the Nazi Party was banned. Most German opinion was against the plotters. Source A gives a view from a newspaper read by people in and around the Ruhr, which was still occupied by the French. The Chancellor, Stresemann, referred to their resistance to the French when he criticised the Putsch in a speech (Source B).

However, Hitler and the small Nazi Party were given little attention in the press until the plotters were tried for high treason in 1924. Through the twenty-four day trial Hitler dominated the courtroom and his photograph and extracts from his defence appeared daily in the papers. Source C is from his closing speech. He was sentenced to five years but had to serve only nine months. His prison suite was stuffed with flowers and presents and he had time to write a book setting out his political ideas – Mein Kampf (My Struggle). After he became Fuehrer the Putsch was commemorated in annual ceremonies. Source D is taken from speeches Hitler made at the 1936 ceremony.

A A view from the Rhine and Ruhr, November 1923

From the depths of our misery on the Rhine, we send to Bavaria a warning and an appeal: control your anger. In so far as you weaken the structure of the Reich, you destroy our confidence here. Bavaria is digging the grave into which the western provinces may well sink.

From Gustav Stresemann, *Diaries, Letters and Papers* (trans. and ed. by Eric Sutton), Macmillan, 1935.

B From a speech by Gustav Stresemann, 1923

It is very regrettable that such events could take place at a time when the population of those parts (the Rhine and the Ruhr) was fighting for its bare life, when all sections of the population were contending against separatist movements and the people were struggling desperately against an oppression that had lasted for many years.

From Gustav Stresemann, *Diaries, Letters and Papers* (trans. and ed. by Eric Sutton), Macmillan, 1935.

C Hitler's defence, 1924

We wanted to create in Germany the precondition which alone will make it possible for the iron grip of our enemies to be removed from us. We wanted to create order in the state, throw out the drones, take up the fight against stock exchange slavery, against our whole economy being cornered by trusts, against the politicizing of the trade unions, and above all, for the highest honourable duty which we, as Germans, know should be once more introduced – the duty of bearing arms, military service. And now I ask you: is what we wanted high treason?

. . . .

From J. Noakes and G. Pridham, *Documents on Nazism*, Jonathan Cape, 1974.

From our bones, from our graves, will sound the voice of that tribunal which alone has the right to sit in judgement upon us. . . . That Court [of History] will judge us . . . as Germans who wanted the best for their people and their fatherland, who wished to fight and to die. You may pronounce us guilty a thousand times, but the Eternal Court of History acquits us.

D Hitler commemorates the Putsch, 1936

The Putsch was the fanatical decision of the young party to build up a New Germany. That was assuredly in the eyes of many an almost insane decision. Certainly at that time there was not a 51 per cent probability of success on our side, but there was a 99 per cent probability in favour of our opponents.

When in 1923 for the first time we determined to act, we had already behind us a long history of preparations for a 'Putsch'. I can confess quite calmly that from 1919–1923 I thought of nothing else. . . . And although we were defeated, this attempt to turn the destiny of Germany was an absolute necessity for one could not talk of revolution for four years and then let the decisive day pass without action. . . . The Government of that day had come to power through violence and it was through violence that it had to be destroyed.

From *The Speeches of Adolph Hitler* (trans. and ed. by N. H. Baynes), OUP 1942.

Questions

1 What did the newspaper (Source A) mean by 'misery on the Rhine'?

2 Why did Stresemann refer to the population of the Rhine and Ruhr 'fighting for its bare life'?

3 Would both the newspaper and Stresemann believe that the Putsch was an act of treason? Explain your answer.

4 Which parts of this 1923 speech were encouraging the German people to break the Treaty of Versailles?

5 What is 'high treason'? Do you think Hitler was guilty of it in 1923?

6 Look at the figures in the first part of Hitler's 1936 speech. Why do you think Hitler gave them?

7 In the second part of Source D, how does Hitler justify the Putsch despite its failure?

8 Suppose the Putsch had been a success and a National Socialist government had taken over in Bavaria. Use Sources A and B to work out the likely reactions of (a) the government in Berlin, (b) the leaders of trade unions in the Ruhr. What might have been the reaction of the French government?

Part 3

Weimar recovery

13 Germany and the Dawes Plan

On 20 November 1923 the German government issued a new currency to bring inflation under control. Everyone could exchange their loads of old, worthless marks for the new rentenmarks. The government then set out to arrange new terms for reparation payments. It believed that the huge sum demanded at Versailles was to blame for the Ruhr occupation and the inflation crisis. An Allied Commission to look into the question was set up, chaired by an American businessman, Charles Dawes.

The negotiations were difficult, partly because the Allies were suspicious about Germany's willingness to pay and partly because many Germans suspected their government was ready for another 'Versailles sell-out'. The outcome in September 1924 was the Dawes Plan for easier reparations instalments and the gradual withdrawal of French troops from the Ruhr.

In a New Year speech, Gustav Stresemann, now foreign minister, explained how the German government saw the need for a new reparations deal (Source A). The American cartoon from the Washington Post (Source B) illustrates the Allied suspicion of Germany's reasons for asking for a new settlement.

A Stresemann on the need for a new reparations deal

From a German point of view we can only be glad that international Commissions should once more conduct investigations into Germany's capacity to pay. We have nothing to conceal. The accusations that were formerly brought against us, that we had consciously worked for the bankruptcy of German finances, can now no longer be maintained. The consequences of Germany's economic collapse are too clear for all to see . . . .

It is clear that in this situation we cannot undertake payments to other countries. It is further clear that we need an international loan that will provide us with the means of supplying our daily needs, of stabilizing our currency, of importing the necessary raw material for our industry, and thus to lay the foundation for a genuine economic prosperity, which alone can bear the burden of German payments in the future. Anyone who wishes to secure payments from Germany in time to come, and is anxious to reckon them in the national budget, must clearly understand that he must first provide Germany with the possibility of making these payments.

From Gustav Stresemann, Diaries, Letters and Papers (trans. and ed. by Eric Sutton), Macmillan, 1935.

From the *Washington Post*, 16 February 1924.

Questions

1 Which country might Stresemann have in mind when he spoke of 'accusations'?

2 What kinds of accusations did the country make against Germany in 1923?

3 What happened during the 'economic collapse' to which Stresemann refers?

4 In your own words, explain what Stresemann wanted the Allies to do to make it possible for Germany to pay reparations in future.

5 What suspicions might a politician in one of the Allied countries shown in the cartoon have had about Stresemann's speech?

6 How does the cartoonist portray the politicians' suspicions?

7 Do you think this cartoon is biased? If so, in which way?

14 Locarno and the League 1925–26

As foreign minister from the end of 1923, Gustav Stresemann worked hard to overcome the widespread distrust of Germany. A first success was the Dawes Plan in 1924. In 1925 he negotiated the Locarno Treaties in which Germany pledged not to change her existing western frontiers. In 1926 Germany became a member of the League of Nations.

Stresemann had to steer a middle course between building good relations with foreign powers and convincing the German people that he was acting strongly in their interests. Source A is from an article he wrote for a French magazine in which he tries to show that Germany was not the wealthy powerful nation many French believed her to be. In a private letter (Source B) to the son of the ex-Kaiser he showed himself more determined to undo the Treaty of Versailles. This was recognised in a letter from Prince Buelow, the war-time Chancellor (Source C).

Stresemann would not have had his successes of 1925 and 1926 without the support of the French foreign minister, Aristide Briand. Source D is part of his speech on Germany entering the League.

A Stresemann defends his country to the French

We see reflected in the eye of France a caricature of Germany that we do not know; a Germany armed and powerful, where there is utter military impotence, imputation* of wealth where we are lamenting the ruined fortunes and lost savings of millions of our fellows. . . . It may be that conditions in Germany are hard to understand for anyone who has not experienced the great change.

From Gustav Stresemann, *Diaries, Letters and Papers* (trans. and ed. by Eric Sutton), Macmillan, 1935.

* *accusation*

B Stresemann reveals his aims

There are three great tasks that confront German foreign policy . . .

From Gustav Stresemann, *Diaries, Letters and Papers* (trans. and ed. by Eric Sutton), Macmillan, 1935.

> In the first place the solution of the Reparations question in a sense tolerable for Germany, and the assurance of peace, which is an essential promise for the recovery of our strength.

> Secondly, the protection of Germans abroad, those 10–12 million of our kindred who live under a foreign yoke in foreign lands.

> The third great task is the readjustment of our Eastern frontiers, the recovery of Danzig, the Polish Corridor, and a correction of the frontier in Upper Silesia.

In the background stands the union with German Austria, although I am quite clear that this not merely brings no advantages to Germany, but seriously complicates the problem of the German Reich . . . .

. . . we are not selling ourselves to the West by joining the League . . . . The most important thing for the first task of German policy mentioned above is the liberation of German soil from any occupying force. We must get the stranglehold off our neck.

C Prince Buelow recognises Stresemann's success

My dear friend,

I cannot let the old year run out without wishing you all that is good in your home and in your work, and, more especially, further political successes. That the Locarno Pact does not fulfil all our just demands and desires, I know . . . But since our collapse, and the shameful Peace of Versailles, you have laid the first stone for peaceful reconstruction. For the first time we were not disposed of, we were treated with; for the first time we were not merely an object. For the first time in seven years the whole world atmosphere has improved . . . .

From Gustav Stresemann, *Diaries, Letter and Papers* (trans. and ed. by Eric Sutton), Macmillan, 1935.

D Support from Briand

It is a striking scene, when, a few years after the most terrible war that has ever swept over the world, while the battlefields are still wet with the blood of the nations, these very nations are present in this peaceful assembly to exchange mutual assurances of a common will to labour together for the peace of the world.

Away with rifles and machine guns and cannons; make place for arbitration and for peace. Herr Stresemann and I have laboured for many months at a common task. I have kept my confidence and so has he.

From Gustav Stresemann, *Diaries, Letters and Papers* (trans. and ed. by Eric Sutton), Macmillan, 1935.

Questions

1 What picture of Germany is Stresemann trying to create in the magazine article? Why do you think he agreed to write it?

2 What might a French person have said in reply to Stresemann's claim that Germany suffered from 'military impotence' and 'ruined fortunes'?

3 Many nationalists felt bitter towards Stresemann. How might his letter to the ex-Crown Prince have changed their opinion?

4 What is the stranglehold that Stresemann writes about in Source B?

5 In Source C what does the Prince mean by not 'disposed of and 'treated with'?

6 Suggest what 'just demands' not fulfilled at Locarno the Prince might have been thinking of.

7 Why was it important that Germany's entry to the League should be welcomed by a Frenchman?

8 How might Briand have felt if he had been able to read Stresemann's letter in Source B?

9 Write a paragraph that Stresemann might have put in his autobiography to defend himself against the charge that the differences between Source A and B show that he was dishonest.

15 Weimar prosperity

By the later 1920s Germany seemed to have recovered her place as one of the world's leading industrial nations. Economic success brought with it political stability. The majority of Germans accepted the Weimar Republic. Risings by the extreme left and right were a thing of the past, and there was no more talk of bringing back the Kaiser.

An election poster (Source A) produced by the German Democratic Party, probably for the elections in December 1924, gives some idea of the uphill struggle it had been against enemies inside Germany and abroad. In 1928 seven British conservative MPs spent 16 days in Germany on a fact-finding tour. On their return they wrote up their findings in a report signed by the group's leader, Sir John Sandelman Allen (Source B).

A The uphill struggle

Imperial War Museum.

B Sir John Sandelman Allen's report

Dealing first with industry . . . from what we saw and heard we were greatly impressed by the fact that industrialists generally were showing great confidence in the future and were laying out capital freely on new works and in reconstructing and adapting old ones . . . .

In some cases at all events they were obtaining capital from abroad especially from America for these purposes. The workpeople appear to be putting in full working hours, while actual working hours are longer and wages paid, we understand, are from 70 per cent to 80 per cent of those paid in this country for shorter work, due no doubt partly to a lower standard of living . . . .

From the London School of Economics Archives: Sir John Sandelman Allen's Report.

Although economic depression and unemployment were spoken of, we were impressed by the fact that even in the thickly populated areas we visited there was very little sign of this. In fact there seemed to be a general air, if not of prosperity, at all events of stability. The iron and steel works were busy with plenty of orders ahead and more hands were being steadily taken on . . . .

We think it may be of interest to record that we found much bitterness in many quarters against the French and in a lesser degree against America . . . . Except, however, in East Prussia and possibly Upper Silesia, where the Polish question is a source of irritation, we found little or no war spirit, indeed we were impressed by the general acceptance of the situation and a determination to make good economy and society, but of course we can only speak of what we ourselves encountered and heard.

It was also interesting to find, even in strong monarchical circles, including leading officials in East Prussia, a general acceptance of the Republican form of government as a necessity for the development of the country, at all events for some time to come . . . .

Questions

1 To which political party do the three figures in the election poster belong?

2 How does the artist show his bias in the way he represents the three figures?

3 To which social class does the central figure belong? How did the two parties throwing stones hope to win the support of this class?

4 How does the poster present a message which is different from those which we are used to in present day elections?

5 Why might some of Germany's neighbours be disturbed by the land mass carried by the central figure?

6 List the signs of Germany's recovery seen by the British visitors.

7 What did they report which might explain why Germany was an attractive country in which to invest?

8 Explain whether or not you are surprised by the bitterness they found towards France.

9 From the rest of the report, why is the reference to bitterness towards America more difficult to understand?

10 Use a map of the post-1919 frontiers of Germany to explain how the Polish question could cause irritation in East Prussia and Upper Silesia.

11 How valuable is the report as evidence of the state of Germany in 1928? Give one argument for it being reliable and one for it being possibly unreliable.

Part 4

The Nazis re-organise, 1925–29

16 Hitler in Landsberg

Hitler was imprisoned in the Landsberg fortress near Munich for his part in the Beer Cellar Putsch. Kurt Ludecke was a close colleague of Hitler at this time. He described a visit to Hitler in prison in his autobiography written in the 1930s (Source A). The first part shows that Hitler had plenty of time to think about the lessons of the Putsch and in the second part Ludecke reports what Hitler told him about his future plans.

In Landsberg Hitler also wrote a political autobiography, Mein Kampf *(My Struggle). Source B shows the frontispiece of an early edition giving its original title. Hitler's publisher had hoped for a best seller to cash in on the publicity Hitler had won at his trial. What he got was so long and badly written that few copies were sold.*

A Hitler in Landsberg

He greeted me with the hearty air of a host receiving a guest . . . . 'Yes, I couldn't be feeling better,' he laughed, showing his old sense of humour. 'This is the first good rest I've ever enjoyed.'

The picture he sketched of a typical day did not strike me as being particularly confining. The prisoners arose at six, breakfasted at seven, walked in the garden from eight until ten. Lunch with his fellow prisoners (some additional 20 members of the unsuccessful coup), with Hitler presiding, sounded more like a social affair. In the afternoon, one prisoner served tea to the others in their cells. Before and after six o'clock supper, which was also served in their cells, they were again free to exercise in the garden for an hour or so. Lights out sounded at ten for all prisoners except Hitler. He was permitted to read and work until midnight or longer . . . .

'From now on,' he said, 'we must follow a new line of action. It is best to attempt no large reorganisation until I am freed, which may be a matter of months rather than years . . . . When I resume active work it will be necessary to pursue a new policy. Instead of working to achieve power by an armed coup, we shall have to hold our noses and enter the Reichstag against the Catholics and Marxist Deputies. If outvoting them takes longer than outshooting them, at least the results will be guaranteed by their own constitution . . . . Sooner or later we shall have a majority – and after that, Germany.'

From Kurt Ludecke, *I knew Hitler*, Charles Scribner's Sons, 1937.

'4½ year struggle against lies, stupidity and cowardice
A Reckoning by Adolf Hitler'

From Adolf Hitler, *Mein Kampf*, F. Eher, 1925.

Translation of insert by photograph:
'Motto
They have to learn to respect each other again. The workers of the brain and the workers of the fist and vice versa have to learn to respect each other. Neither one would exist without the other, out of them the new man has to crystallise, the man of the coming German Empire.

Adolf Hitler'

Questions

1 Why does Ludecke's account make it difficult to believe that Hitler was in prison at Landsberg?

2 Why do you think he was allowed such unusual privileges?

3 Explain in your own words what Hitler's new policy described to Ludecke was to be.

4 What might have been Ludecke's main purpose in writing his essay? Does this affect its value as a source on the early Hitler movement?

5 What kind of image of Hitler was the publisher probably trying to create with the photograph?

6 Who do you think Hitler had in mind when he spoke of his struggle against 'lies, stupidity and cowardice' in the original title of his book?

7 What do you think was Hitler's purpose in writing his autobiography when he was such a relatively unknown figure?

8 What is the special value of such a book to the historian?

17 The Fuehrer in waiting, 1925

Hitler was released from prison in December 1924. He planned to reform his banned Nazi Party but circumstances were much less in his favour than at the time of the Beer Cellar Putsch. In Source A, Kurt Ludecke gives three reasons why the German people were less likely to turn to national socialism in 1925 and 1926 than they had been in 1923 and 1924.

However, Hitler persuaded the Bavarian government to lift the ban on his party and its newspaper. He then re-founded the party at a meeting in the beer cellar where the failed Putsch had begun. Four thousand of the old faithful turned up to cheer his two hour speech (Source B) in which Hitler left them in no doubt that he intended to be the party's sole leader.

Soon afterwards he was banned from public speaking in Germany and so he concentrated on writing a second volume of Mein Kampf *while officials ran the party. In his autobiography (Source C), Ernst Hanfstaengl makes it clear how difficult Hitler made this for them. Yet he kept a group of devoted supporters, as Kurt Ludecke recalled in his autobiography (Source D).*

A National Socialism out of favour

The three principal circumstances which had helped the Nazi Party to gain a strong hold on the masses were no longer effective. First, Mussolini's triumph in Italy, which had made a tremendous impression on the German mind, was no longer news. Second, the Ruhr invasion, now that the French had withdrawn and Hitler had failed as an avenging angel, was no longer a burning issue; it had been half-forgotten though the wound was still open. Third, and of prime importance, the inflation was over and the re-established mark had brought to the country a general but evanescent* relief. The middle class and especially the peasants believed their insecurity ended ... the international 'experts' brought a flood of foreign gold into the country, creating a mock prosperity which actually lasted several years and fooled the majority of the plain citizens.

From Kurt Ludecke, *I knew Hitler*, Charles Scribner's Sons, 1937.

* *short-lived*

B Hitler re-founds the Nazi Party, February 1925

At the end of a year you shall judge, my comrades. If I have acted rightly, well and good. If I have acted wrongly I shall resign my office into your hands. Until then, however, I alone lead the movement, and no one can impose conditions on me so long as I personally bear the responsibility. And I once more bear the whole responsibility for everything that occurs in the movement .... To this struggle of ours there are only two possible issues; either the enemy pass over our bodies or we pass over theirs, and it is my desire that, if in the struggle I should fall, the Swastika banner shall be my winding sheet.

From R. T. Clark, *The Fall of the German Republic*, London, 1935.

C Hitler as leader

Hitler himself lived a shadowy existence and it was very difficult to keep track of his movements. He had the Bohemian habits of a man who had grown up with no real roots. He was hopelessly unpunctual and incapable of keeping to any sort of schedule . . . .

He never stopped talking all day, committed nothing to paper, issued no directives and was the despair of his staff. He would make appointments and never be there, or would be discovered somewhere looking at second-hand motor cars.

From Ernst Hanfstaengl, *Hitler: The Missing Years*, Eyre and Spottiswoode, 1957.

D Hitler and his followers

. . . he was surrounded chiefly by men like himself and not by people who were rich or highly educated . . . . They were men from the most modest homes, like his own, who knew nothing of the great world beyond their home towns, but were sincere, enthusiastic, loyal, looking upon Hitler as not only a genius but an inspired prophet. To understand these men was largely to understand Hitler and his power.

Night after night he sat in their little homes or in the simpler cafés of Munich, expounding his doctrines. His listeners adored him. The fact that he was one of them, not a man from above, sealed their devotion. They hung on his every word, hardly interrupting even with a question. They were his circle of disciples, ready to do or die for him.

From Kurt Ludecke, *I knew Hitler*, Charles Scribner's Sons, 1937.

Questions

1 Find the three circumstances which Kurt Ludecke believed were no longer helping the Nazi Party (Source A). For each one give its date and add a sentence explaining why it had, at the time, helped the Nazis gain popularity.

2 What hint can you find in Source A that the situation might again turn in the Nazis' favour?

3 Suppose you are with a friend in the beer cellar listening to Hitler's speech in Source B. You are both in favour of reforming the Party, but you are unhappy with Hitler's plans for leadership while your friend believes he should be sole leader. Improvise or write out a conversation.

4 Think of an embarrassing situation which might have arisen because of Hitler's style of leadership described in Source C.

5 After reading Source C, can you think why the men described in Source D were so devoted to Hitler?

6 What reasons does Source D suggest for Hitler feeling so much at ease with such men?

7 How do you think Hitler might have been affected by being constantly in the company of such 'disciples'?

18 The SA at work, 1926–29

The later 1920s were the years when the Nazi Party built a nation-wide network of fanatical party workers backed by squads of brownshirts, the SA, or Sturmabteilung. The SA had been disbanded after the failure of the Munich Putsch but it was re-formed in the autumn of 1926.

Source A gives one of Hitler's orders to the SA which makes clear their task as strong-arm support for Party propaganda workers. Source B, which is part of an essay written for a competition in 1934 to find the best life-history of a supporter of the Hitler movement, shows this in practice. A Nazi bank clerk recalls how the SA protected a Nazi supporter who risked losing business from followers of other parties. Source C is a propaganda poster of the re-formed SA. Compare it with the photograph (Source D) of SA men at the time of the Munich Putsch.

A SA Order 111, 1 November 1926

The SA man is the holy freedom fighter. The member of the Party is the clever propagandist and skilled agitator. Political propaganda tries to enlighten the opponent, to argue with him, to understand his point of view, to enter into his thoughts, to agree with him to a certain extent. But when the SA arrives on the scene this stops. It makes no concessions. It goes all out. It only recognises the motto (metaphorically): Kill or be killed.

From J. Noakes and G. Pridham, *Documents on Nazism*, Jonathan Cape, 1974.

B The story of a bank clerk

Master carpenter Thersky was the first Rastenburg citizen to find the courage at that time [1929] to put his furniture storeroom, holding a few hundred people, at the disposal of the party . . . . In return he was exposed to a boycott by the adherents of the left, and indeed, even of the bourgeoisie. Often stones were thrown at his house, and demonstrations were a daily occurrence. The SA of the whole district acted as a guard for the hall at the first and second meetings. When we finally succeeded in carrying on the meetings in safety to the participants, the ground was cleared. The press printed half-way decent notices and we were able to hire a hall in the city. To be sure, we had to pay an excessive rent and besides be responsible for damages. You shall hear what that means. The three battles which took place in the hall cost us more than 800 marks in damages. The day following every meeting a collection had to be taken up. Contributions of a mark, really made with difficulty, sufficed in a few days to cover our bills. And we must never forget to thank our SA who beforehand distributed handbills and sold tickets for days and afterwards had to do the fighting. The SA of Korschen won everlasting laurels. Workmen, students, artisans, office employees, and unemployed formed the 'mass' of the small but determined SA of that time.

From Theodore Abel, *Why Hitler came to Power*, Prentice Hall, 1938.

C SA recruiting poster

D The SA Munich Regiment 1923

Questions

1 If you had been an ordinary member of the SA in 1926 what would you have thought Hitler expected of you, according to Source A?

2 What impression of the SA was Hitler trying to create by putting in the 'metaphorically' in the last line of Order 111?

3 What is the evidence from Source B that you had to be either brave or foolish to let the Nazis use your property for meetings?

4 Who did the writer of Source B probably have in mind when he spoke of the 'adherents of the left'?

5 Using Source B, make a list of all the activities expected of a local SA member.

6 Does your list support or confirm Hitler's Order 111? Explain.

7 How can you tell that the photograph (Source D) was taken not long after the First World War? What does it reveal about the kind of men who joined the early SA?

8 How does the poster (Source C) create a very different image of the SA?

9 Imagine that the bank clerk of Source B was trying to get you to join the local SA branch. How would you respond?

Part 5

The Nazis win support, 1929–33

19 The Wall Street Crash and economic crisis

In October 1929 the President of the Reichsbank, Hjalmar Schacht, was attending a conference on Germany's reparations problems chaired by an American, Owen D. Young. It eventually reduced the reparations to about one-quarter of the original sum. In his autobiography in 1955, Schacht recalls how the news broke of the crash on Wall Street (Source A).

Some years later, in June 1934, Victor Schiff, a leading Social Democrat, who had had to flee Hitler's Germany, wrote an article for an international magazine expressing the view that the Nazis would never have come to power had it not been for the Wall Street Crash and the depression that followed (Source B).

The experience of one small town in Northern Germany called Northeim gives some idea of how the depression hit Germany. Firstly, unemployment soared (Source C). When the town council could not make ends meet, there were cuts in pensions, the dole and even in wages. Disturbances happened daily in this once sleepy place (Source D).

A Americans and the Crash

Right in the middle of the conference there burst the Wall Street Crash.

When Jackson Reynolds (a New York banker) approached the breakfast table one morning I felt compelled to remark, 'Mr Jackson, you don't look very cheerful. What's the matter?'

'Haven't you seen the despatches from New York?'

'Of course I have. But surely it won't hit you very much?'

'Unfortunately it hits me very seriously as I have large commitments on Wall Street.'

A few minutes later Mr Taylor (a Chicago banker) came in with a beaming face, waving his daily wire from New York.

'Seen the reports from New York, Dr Schacht?'

'Certainly. How has it hit you?'

'It hasn't hit me at all. When I left New York for Europe on a visit of several weeks I sold all my securities like the far-sighted man I am.'

Jackson's face grew longer and longer, Taylor's grin broader and broader.

From Hjalmar Schacht, *My First Seventy-Six Years* (trans. Diana Pyke), Alan Wingate, 1955.

B The consequences for Germany

If there is indeed a point on which there is . . . no difference of opinion among us, it must surely be that Hitler owes his rise and his ultimate victory essentially to the World Economic Crisis: to the despair of the unemployed proletariat; to the academically trained youth for whom there is no future; to the middle class businessman and craftsman heading for bankruptcy and to the farmers threatened with a fall in agricultural prices. In this connection, all of us have indeed been found wanting . . . we were not in a position to offer the masses anything more than mere socialistic phrases.

Victor Schiff, quoted in Hjalmar Schacht, *My First Seventy-Six Years* (trans. Diana Pyke), Alan Wingate, 1955.

C Northeim: registered unemployed

1930 —   392 unemployed
1931 — 12,000 unemployed
1932 — 14,000 unemployed

From W. S. Allen, *The Nazi Seizure of Power*, Franklin Watts, 1984.

D Northeimer Stop Press, December 6 1932

I am hungry! I have hunger and nothing else!

Shouted by an unemployed worker arrested for disturbing the peace and refusing to move from the Welfare Office.

From W. S. Allen, *The Nazi Seizure of Power*, Franklin Watts, 1984.

Questions

1 What do you understand by the 'Crash' on the Wall Street stock market?

2 How can you tell from Source A that news of the Wall Street Crash caught most people by surprise?

3 Explain what has happened on Wall Street to make Mr Jackson Reynolds so miserable.

4 In what way might 'far-sighted' men such as Mr Taylor have helped bring about the crash in the first place?

5 Use Victor Schiff's article (Source B) to show how the Wall Street Crash affected

the following groups in Germany: (a) workers; (b) students; (c) businessmen; (d) farmers.

6 What does Victor Schiff feel guilty about?

7 What do the figures for unemployment in Northeim tell you?

8 If you were still in work in Northeim in 1931 what would be your feelings as you considered these figures?

9 Work in groups of three, using Sources C and D to design recruiting posters for the local (a) NSDAP, (b) Communist Party, (c) Social Democratic Party.

20 The Nazi propaganda machine

One of Hitler's central interests was propaganda, as Kurt Ludecke, one of his early advisers, recalls in Source A. All parties used propaganda to get their message across but Nazi propaganda was specially noted for its skill in appealing to feelings and prejudices rather than parliamentary issues. At election time, Nazi propaganda reached fever-pitch with posters (Source C), parades, mass meetings, door-to-door leafleting, torchlight processions, firework displays and even family shows.

All these activities were directed by the Party's propaganda department which decided what the main themes and slogans were to be but then let local officials adapt them. From April 1930 Joseph Goebbels was chief of Nazi propaganda. His orders for the Presidential election of spring 1932 show how everything was planned to the last detail (Source B).

A Hitler's 'strongest point'?

Only one thing was managed marvellously from the beginning – the propaganda, Hitler's personal hobby and perhaps his strongest point. He had a matchless instinct for taking advantage of every breeze to raise a political whirlwind. No official scandal was so petty that he could not magnify it into high treason; he could ferret out the most deviously ramified* corruption in high places and plaster the town with the bad news. He shone in print and positively dazzled on the lecture platform.

From Kurt Ludecke, *I knew Hitler*, Charles Scribner's Sons, 1937.

* *branching-out*

B Propaganda Department Instruction, 1932 Presidential Elections for Regional Departments

(1) . . . *A striking slogan:*
Those who want everything to stay as it is vote for Hindenburg. Those who want everything changed vote for Hitler.

From J. Noakes and G. Pridham, *Documents on Nazism*, Jonathan Cape, 1974.

(2) . . . *Hitler Poster:*
The Hitler poster depicts a fascinating Hitler head on a completely black background. Subtitle: white on black – 'Hitler'. In accordance with the Fuehrer's wish this poster is to be put up only during the final days. Since experience shows that during the final days there is a variety of coloured posters, this poster with its completely black background will contrast with all the others and will produce a tremendous effect on the masses . . . .

(3) *For the National Socialist Press*
1. From Easter Tuesday 29 March until Saturday 10 April inclusive, all National Socialist papers, both daily and weekly, must appear in an enlarged edition with a tripled circulation. Two-thirds of this tripled circulation must be made available, without charge, to the Gau* lead-

* *local district*

ership responsible for its area of distribution for propaganda purposes . . . .

2. From Easter Tuesday 29 March until Sunday 3 April inclusive, a special topic must be dealt with every day on the first page of all our papers in a big spread. Tuesday 29 March: Hitler as a man. Wednesday 30 March: Hitler as a fighter (gigantic achievements through his willpower, etc). Friday April 2: Hitler as a statesman – plenty of photos . . . .

3. On Sunday 3 April, at noon . . . . the great propaganda journey of the Fuehrer through Germany will start, through our Fuehrer's speeches . . . the press organisation is planned so that four press centres will be set up in Germany, which in turn will pass on immediately any telephone calls to the other papers of their area, whose names have been given them . . . .

C Ought he to get still fatter?

'We give our vote to the National Socialist German Workers' Party. Vote Hitler'

Questions

1 What does Source A suggest was the aim of Hitler's propaganda?

2 What insight into Hitler's character does Source A give us?

3 Study the poster (Source C).
  (a) Which party is it attacking?
  (b) To which party is it appealing?

4 How does the poster use a stereotype to damage the reputation of its opponents?

5 Who or what is the little figure in the bottom left-hand corner supposed to represent?

6 Does the poster comply with Goebbels' recommendation (1) in Source B? Explain your answer.

7 For what effect is Goebbels striving in his instructions about the Hitler poster? What does this reveal about the way propaganda works?

8 What kind of an image is Goebbels trying to create for Hitler through the newspapers in Source B (2)?

9 How important a role does Source B (3) suggest newspapers would have in this election, and can you think of any reasons for this?

10 Do you think *any* message can be got across through propaganda or is there a limit on its power? If so, what do you think makes the limit?

21 The Nazi breakthrough, 1930

Between 1928 and 1930 there were twelve Nazi members of the German parliament, or Reichstag, and fifty-four Communists, compared with nearly 350 Reichstag members who wished to see Germany governed democratically. In September 1930 the government of the Centre Party leader, Heinrich Bruening, called an election. His election poster (Source C) shows his party's concern that the anti-democratic parties would do well.

Source A shows how right these worries were. It is from the diary of Count Harry Kessler, the son of a German father and Irish mother who was educated in France and England and became a journalist. He was nicknamed the 'Red Count' because he was known as a supporter of the German Democratic Party. His view was echoed by a cartoon (Source B) of early 1931 in the Social Democratic Party newspaper. The Nazis' reasons for fighting elections are set out in an article (Source D) which Joseph Goebbels, their propaganda chief, had written before the 1928 elections.

A A view of the results, 15 September 1930

A black day for Germany. The Nazis have increased the number of their seats almost tenfold, from 12 to 107, and have become the second largest party in the Reichstag. The impression created abroad must be catastrophic. The repercussion on foreign and financial affairs is likely to be appalling. A hundred and seven Nazis, 41 Hugenberg supporters* and more than 70 Communists total some 220 deputies who are radical opponents of the German state in its present shape and want to do away with it by revolutionary means. We face a national crisis which can only be overcome if all those who accept, or at least tolerate, the Republic stand firmly together.

From Count Harry Kessler, *The Diaries of a Cosmopolitan* (trans. C. Kessler), Weidenfeld and Nicolson, 1971.

* Nationalists sympathetic to Hitler

B Hitler's advance — a socialist warning

Wie seit dem 14. September 1930 die National-sozialistische Partei ihrem Ziel ständig näher kommt!

'Since 14 September 1930 the National Socialist Party has moved closer to its goal.'

From *Vorwaerts*, 28 April 1931.

C Centre Party election poster, September 1930

'Bruening for freedom and order: the last defence of truth, freedom, justice'

D Goebbels reveals Nazi aims, 1928

We go into the Reichstag in order to acquire the weapons of democracy from its arsenal. We become Reichstag deputies in order to paralyze the Weimar democracy with its own assistance. If democracy is stupid enough to give us free travel privileges and per diem* allowances for this service, that is its affair .... We'll take any legal means to revolutionize the existing situation. If we succeed in putting 60 to 70 agitators of our party into the various parliaments in these elections, then in future the state itself will supply and finance our fighting machinery .... We come as enemies. Like the wolf tearing into the flock of sheep, that is how we come.

From Karl Dietrich Baracher, *The German Dictatorship*, Penguin, 1973.

* *daily*

Questions

1 What is the Bruening poster (Source C) asking the voter to vote *for* and *against*?

2 What other everyday issues might have been on a voter's mind at this time?

3 Suggest a way the poster might have back-fired and made the opponents look more attractive than the government.

4 How does Count Kessler reveal his attitude towards the Nazi Party in Source A?

5 What reasons does he give for this attitude?

6 What 'repercussions' might Kessler have been thinking of which could have been appalling for Germany?

7 What is the sting in the tail of the scorpion that the Social Democratic cartoon warns against?

8 Use examples from Goebbels' article to show whether he contradicts or confirms Kessler and the poster.

9 Who are the 'sheep' to which Goebbels refers at the end of Source D? What picture did he intend that the word should bring into a reader's mind?

22 The mass rallies

In 1932 there were three national elections: one for the Presidency in April; one for the Reichstag in July; and yet another for the Reichstag in November. These provided the newly successful Nazi Party with targets for their agitation.

The centerpiece of the Nazi election campaigns were their mass rallies. Back in 1924, in Mein Kampf, *Hitler pointed out the psychological impact of such occasions (Source A). Ernst Hanfstaengl, one of Hitler's earliest patrons, recollected in his autobiography, written in the 1950s, how thoroughly Hitler prepared for such occasions (Source B).*

Kurt Ludecke was in Berlin in 1932 for the famous Gruenwald Stadium Rally. At the time he was one of Hitler's closest political advisers. Later, he was to fall out with Hitler and was put in a concentration camp. In 1937 he wrote his autobiography (Source C) after his escape to America.

A Adolf Hitler on mass suggestion

The mass meeting is also necessary for the reason that in it the individual who at first, while becoming a supporter of a young movement, feels lonely and easily succumbs to the fear of being alone, for the first time gets the picture of a larger community, which in most people has a strengthening, encouraging effect . . . . When from his little workshop or big factory, in which he feels very small, he steps for the first time into a mass meeting and has thousands and thousands of people of the same opinions around him, when, as a seeker, he is swept away by three or four thousand others into the mighty effect of suggesting intoxication and enthusiasm, when the visible success and agreement of thousands confirm to him the rightness of the new doctrine . . . then he himself has succumbed to the magic influence of what we designate as 'mass suggestion'.

From Adolf Hitler, *Mein Kampf* (trans. R. Manheim), Hutchinson, 1974.

B Hitler's preparations for a rally

Hitler suffered no one in the room when he was working on his speeches. In the early years he did not dictate them as he did later. It took him between four and six hours to block one out on large foolscap sheets, about ten or twelve in number, with, in the end, only fifteen or twenty words on each as a cue. When the hour of the meeting approached he used to walk up and down the room as though rehearsing in his mind the various phrases of his argument. During this time the telephone would keep ringing . . . to tell Hitler how things were going in the hall. He would ask how many people there were, what their mood was or whether much opposition was to be expected. He would give continuous directions concerning the handling of the audience while they were waiting for him and, half an hour after the meeting had started, would call for his overcoat, whip and hat and go out to the car preceded by his bodyguard and chauffeur . . . .

From Ernst Hanfstaengl, *Hitler: The Missing Years*, Eyre and Spottiswoode, 1957.

When he had finished [speaking] the band used to play the national anthem. Hitler would salute to right and left and leave while the music was being played. He had usually reached his car before the singing was over. This sudden withdrawal had a number of advantages . . . . He once said to me: 'Most speakers make the great mistake of hanging around after their speech is over. This only leads to anticlimax.

C The Gruenwald Stadium Rally – July 1932

More than a hundred thousand people had paid to squeeze inside, while another hundred thousand packed a nearby race-track where loud-speakers had been set up to carry Hitler's words. And at home millions were waiting at the radio . . . .

From Kurt Ludecke, *I knew Hitler*, Charles Scribner's Sons, 1937.

Around the entire perimeter of the vast stone arena, banners were silhouetted against the darkening sky. Row under row, the seats stepped down to the centre field . . . . Directly opposite reared a dramatic speaking-stand, its bold, cubical masses hung with giant swastikas which gained significance through sheer magnification. Draperies likewise flaunting swastikas made a simple and thrilling background. Picked men from the Schutz-staffel* were drawn up in close ranks below the stand. Twelve huge SA bands played military marches with beautiful precision and terrifying power. Behind the bands, on the field itself, solid squares of uniformed men from the Nazi labour unions were ranged in strict military order, thousands strong . . . .

* protection squads

Suddenly . . . a word was tossed from man to man: Hitler is coming! Hitler is here! A blare of trumpets rent the air, and a hundred thousand people leaped to their feet in tense expectancy. All eyes were turned towards the stand, awaiting the approach of the Fuehrer. There was a low rumble of excitement and then, releasing its pent-up emotion, the crowd burst into a tremendous ovation, the 'Heils' swelling until they were like the roar of a mighty cataract.

Questions

1 Does Hitler's description of the impact of a mass meeting show a good understanding of human nature?

2 How do you think the way Hitler prepared his speeches (Source B) influenced the sort of speeches he made?

3 How important a role does Source B suggest Hitler played in the management of rallies?

4 List the propaganda devices mentioned by Kurt Ludecke in Source C.

5 Do you think that the process described in Source A was likely to be achieved at a rally like the one in C?

23 Masters of the streets

The Nazi Party's rise to power via the ballot box took place in an atmosphere of increasing violence. Most of the political parties had strong-arm squads to protect their meetings and break up those of their opponents. By the spring of 1932, Germany seemed to some to be on the verge of civil war. This situation is illustrated in a cartoon of the time by Karl Arnold (Source A).

Hitler stressed that he wanted fighters, not just supporters, in the first order which he issued to the Nazi Party's private army, the SA, after it was re-formed in 1926 (Source B). Both Count Harry Kessler and Christopher Isherwood were living in Berlin in the early 1930s. Kessler, a political journalist, kept a diary. Source C is his entry for the day the Reichstag met after the elections of 1930 (see Unit 21). Later, Isherwood included an incident he witnessed then in his novel Goodbye to Berlin, *which was published in 1939 (Source D).*

A   Cartoon by Karl Arnold, 1932

'*If this goes on any longer the only army we will have left will be the Salvation Army.*'

B SA Order 1: 1 November 1926

What we need is not a hundred or two hundred daring conspirators, but a hundred thousand and hundreds of thousands more fanatical fighters . . . : We have to teach Marxism that National Socialism is the future master of the streets, just as it will one day be master of the state.

(signed) Adolf Hitler

From J. Noakes and G. Pridham, *Documents on Nazism*, Jonathan Cape, 1974.

C Count Kessler's diary, 13 October 1930

Reichstag opening. The whole afternoon and evening mass demonstrations by the Nazis. During the afternoon they smashed the windows of Wertheim, Gruenfeld and other department stores in the Leipzigerstrasse . . . the mischief was organised. Only businesses with Jewish names suffered.

From Count Harry Kessler, *The Diaries of a Cosmopolitan* (trans. C. Kessler), Weidenfeld and Nicolson, 1971.

D Isherwood: a street incident, 1932

There had been a big Nazi meeting at the Sportplast and groups of men and boys were just coming away from it, in their brown or black uniforms. Walking along the pavement ahead of me were three SA men. They all carried Nazi banners on their shoulders, like rifles, rolled tight round the staves – the banner staves had sharp metal points, shaped into arrowheads.

All at once, the three SA men came face to face with a youth of seventeen or eighteen, dressed in civilian clothes, who was hurrying along in the opposite direction. I heard one of the Nazis shout: 'That's him!' and immediately all three of them flung themselves upon the young man, He uttered a scream, and tried to dodge, but they were too quick for him. In a moment they had jostled him into the shadow of a house entrance, and were standing over him, kicking and stabbing at him with the sharp metal points of their banners. All this happened with such incredible speed that I could hardly believe my eyes – already the three SA men had left their victim, and were barging their way through the crowd . . . .

Another passer-by and myself were the first to reach the doorway where the young man was lying. He lay huddled crookedly in the corner, like an abandoned sack. As they picked him up, I got a sickening glimpse of his face – his left eye was poked half out, and blood poured from the wound . . . .

By this time, dozens of people were looking on. They seemed surprised, but not particularly shocked . . . . Twenty yards away stood a group of heavily armed policemen. With their chests out, and their hands on their revolver belts, they magnificently disregarded the whole affair.

From Christopher Isherwood, *Goodbye to Berlin*, Penguin, 1969.

Questions

1 To what event in Nazi history is Hitler referring when he writes of 'conspirators' in Source B? Why did he think the party now needed 'hundreds of thousands' of fighters?

2 Which party did Hitler consider to be his main rival?

3 To what political parties do the remains of the three armies shown in the cartoon belong?

4 How did you identify them?

5 What do you think is the cartoon's political message?

6 Why do you think the Nazis demonstrated so violently on the day the Reichstag opened (Source C)?

7 What evidence is there in Source C that the Nazis were anti-semitic?

8 Is there anything in Source D to suggest that violence was probably expected by the men in brown and black uniforms?

9 What might you learn about Germany at this time from the attitude of the bystanders?

10 For what *two* different reasons might the police have ignored the incident?

11 Give one advantage and one disadvantage of using novels as evidence for the past even when, as in this case, the incidents described were actually witnessed by the writer.

24 The respectable face of Nazism

By 1931 Hitler and many German leaders of business and industry were beginning to realise that they could be of great use to each other. Hitler needed their influential contacts and funds; they wanted strong leadership to rebuild Germany's economy and were attracted by the Nazis' determination to smash Marxism.

Hjalmar Schacht had been President of the Reichsbank in the 1920s. In 1931 he met Hitler at a dinner party. Later he became Economics Minister in the Nazi government. He recalls the dinner party in his autobiography (Source A).

On 27 January 1931 Hitler was invited to speak to influential businessmen at the Industry Club at Duesseldorf. It was the first time that many of the industrialists had met Hitler and they gave him a cool reception. He won them over, however, in a two and a half hour speech. Source B gives some idea of its contents.

Businessmen were still disturbed by the Nazis' violent behaviour, but they believed that these could be dealt with once Hitler was working for them. The 1933 cartoon drawn soon after Hitler became Chancellor reflects this belief.

A Hjalmar Schacht at Goering's dinner party

Hitler came in after dinner. He wore dark trousers and the traditional yellowish-brown jacket – the uniform of the party. His appearance was neither pretentious nor affected – on the contrary he was natural and unassuming .... After the many rumours that we had heard about Hitler and the published criticism we had read of him we were pleasantly impressed by the general atmosphere.

Our talk quickly turned to political and economic problems. At this first meeting I learned that in discussion with Hitler his associates contributed only five percent; Hitler himself supplied the remaining ninety-five percent of the conversation .... He spoke with moderation and was obviously anxious to avoid anything that might shock us ...

The thing that impressed me most about this man was his absolute conviction of the rightness of his outlook and his determination to translate this outlook into practical action.

From Hjalmar Schacht, My First Seventy-Six Years (trans. Diana Pyke), Alan Wingate, 1955.

B Hitler addresses the Industry Club

Here is an organization which ... when a political opponent says, 'Your behaviour we regard as a provocation,' does not see fit immediately to retire from the scene, but brutally enforces its own will and hurls against the opponent the retort: 'We fight today! We fight tomorrow!' ... yes, we have formed the inexorable decision to destroy Marxism in Germany down to its very last root ....

I know quite well, gentlemen, that when National Socialists march through the streets and suddenly in the evening there arises a tumult and a commotion, then the bourgeois draws back the window-curtain, looks out, and says: 'Once again my night's rest is disturbed: no more sleep for me. Why must these Nazis always be so provocative and run

From The Speeches of Adolph Hitler (trans. and ed. by N. H. Baynes), OUP, 1942.

about the place at night?' . . . But remember that it means sacrifice when today many hundreds of thousands of SA and SS men of the National Socialist movement have every day to mount on their lorries, protect meetings, undertake marches, sacrifice themselves night after night and then come back in the grey dawn to workshop and factory, or as unemployed to take their pittance of the dole: it means sacrifice when from the little they possess they have further to buy their uniforms, their shirts, their badges, yes, and even pay their own fares. Believe me, there is already in all this force an ideal – a great ideal! And if the whole German nation today possessed this idealism, Germany would stand in the eyes of the world otherwise than she stands now! (loud applause)

C   The new Chancellor: sitting uncomfortably

'*Even when you are warm, you may often be uncomfortable!*'

From *Der Wahre Jacob*, 4 March 1933.

Questions

1 For what reasons might Source A not be entirely reliable?

2 How does Hitler appear to have been making an effort to appeal to Goering's respectable guests?

3 What seems to have impressed Schacht so much about Hitler?

4 Why might the industrialists. be pleased to hear Hitler's views on 'Marxism'?

5 Show how Hitler tries to reduce their fears.

6 In the cartoon what does the chair represent?

7 How does the cartoon portray Hitler differently from the other two sources?

8 Who are the figures beneath his chair and what are they up to?

9 Suggest a design for a cartoon which shows that businessmen were mistaken in believing they would control Hitler.

25 Why I became a Nazi

By 1932 the Nazis were trying to appeal to as wide a cross section of German society as possible. Their election propaganda included something for everyone except for the Jews, who were always made the scapegoat for Germany's misery.

Frau Luise Solmitz, an upper-middle-class school teacher who lived in Hamburg, kept a diary. Her entry for 23 April 1932 (Source A) shows how easily people got caught up in a kind of mass adoration of Hitler.

Maria Habenichts and Kurt Zeisser both lived in Northeim in North Germany in 1932. She was a thirty-seven-year-old housewife and he a fifteen-year-old printer's apprentice. Later, in the early 1960s, they were interviewed in the United States by an historian about their reasons for becoming Nazis (Sources B and C).

The same historian received a letter in 1967 from Dr Edmund Venzlaff, who had joined the Nazi Party in 1932. He was the headmaster of a girls' high school at the time and recalls his reasons for turning to the Nazis (Source D).

A The school teacher at a rally, 1932

The April sun shone hot like in summer and turned everything into a picture of gay expectations. There was immaculate order and discipline. . . . In the background, at the edge of the track, there were columns of carriers like ammunition carriers. What they carried were crates of beer. Aeroplanes above us. Testing of the loud speakers, buzzing of the cine-cameras. It was nearly 3 pm. 'The Fuehrer is coming!' A ripple went through the crowds. Around the speaker's platform one could see hands raised in the Hitler salute . . . . A second speaker welcomed Hitler and made way for the man who had drawn 120,000 people of all classes and ages. There stood Hitler in a simple black coat and looked over the crowd, waiting – a forest of swastika pennants swished up, the jubilation of this moment was given vent in a roaring salute . . . . His voice was hoarse after all his speaking during the previous days. When the speech was over, there was roaring enthusiasm and applause . . . . How many look up to him with touching faith as their helper, their saviour, their deliverer from unbearable distress – to him who rescues the Prussian prince, the scholar, the clergyman, the farmer, the worker, the unemployed, who raises them from the parties back into the nation.

From J. Noakes and G. Pridham, *Documents of Nazism*, Jonathan Cape, 1974.

B The housewife

The ranks of the NSDAP were filled with young people. Those serious people who joined did so because they were for social justice, or opposed to unemployment. There was a feeling of restless energy about the Nazis. You constantly saw the swastika painted on the sidewalks or found them littered by pamphlets put out by the Nazis. I was drawn by the feeling of strength about the party, even though there was much in it that was highly questionable.

From W. S. Allen, *The Nazi Seizure of Power*, Franklin Watts, 1984.

C The printer's apprentice

It was the depression and business was bad. The Nazis used to ask my father for contributions and he refused. As a consequence of this he lost business. So he joined the Nazi Party. But this lost him other customers, so he was discouraged by the whole situation. He probably wouldn't have joined of his own choice.

From W. S. Allen, *The Nazi Seizure of Power*, Franklin Watts, 1984.

D The headmaster

I saw the Communist danger, the Communist terror, their gangs breaking up 'Bourgeois' meetings, the 'Bourgeois' parties being utterly helpless, the Nazis being the only party that broke terror by anti-terror. I saw the complete failure of the 'Bourgeois' parties to deal with the economic crisis (6 to 7 millions out of work, the Reichsbank discount up to 15 per cent). Only national socialism offered any hope. Anti-semitism had another aspect in Berlin; Nazis mostly did not hate Jews individually, many had Jewish friends but they were concerned about the Jewish problem: most Jews, though ready for complete assimilation, willing to be 100 per cent Germans, persisted in being loyal to their Jewish fellows (mostly coming in from Poland and Russia), helping them, pushing them on, so that more and more Jews got positions not only in trade, banking, theatre, film, the newspapers, etc, whole branches of the economy and key positions being in the hands of Jews, also doctors, lawyers, etc. Many people saw the danger of that problem. Nobody knew any way to deal with it, but they hoped the Nazis would know. If they had guessed how the Nazis did deal with it, not one in a hundred would have joined the party.

From W. S. Allen, *The Nazi Seizure of Power*, Franklin Watts, 1984.

Questions

1 What evidence is there in Source A that the rally was carefully stage-managed?

2 The majority of converts to Nazism say that they were first won over on occasions like this. What clues does Frau Solmitz give us as to the reasons why this was so?

3 In your own words explain what she means by 'raises them from the parties back into the nation'.

4 What circumstance is mentioned in both Sources B and C as an ingredient in the situation that made Nazism attractive?

5 What does Source D suggest about the political outlook of the headmaster?

6 Was he attracted to the Nazis by similar factors to those described in B and C?

7 Write a letter back to this headmaster. Begin by pointing out that the chief occupation of Jews in the 1930s was tailoring. Attack the false reasoning in his letter.

Part 6

The Nazis take power, 1933–34

26 The Reichstag fire, February 1933

In January 1933 Hitler was made Chancellor, heading a coalition of Nationalists and Nazis. Socialist and Communist members together outnumbered Nazis in the Reichstag. Hitler was determined that his party should be in sole power after elections in March.

On 27 February the Reichstag building was burned down. The police found a young Communist, Marinus van der Lubbe, in the ruins. Hitler claimed there was a Communist plot. He ordered the arrest of all Communists and put the press and public meetings under government control. In the elections the Nazis won a large majority. Historians do not agree on who was responsible for the fire or whether, if van der Lubbe did start it, it was the result of his being mentally ill.

Rudolf Diels was the police chief called to the fire. After the war he gave the account in Source A. A Punch *cartoon expressed the suspicions of many outside Germany.*

A   The police chief's view

A few officers of my department were already engaged in interrogating Marinus van der Lubbe. Naked from the waist upwards, smeared with dirt and sweating, he sat in front of them, breathing heavily. He panted as if he had completed a tremendous task. I sat opposite him in the police headquarters several times that night and listened to his confused stories. I read the Communist pamphlets he carried . . . .

Shortly after my arrival in the burning Reichstag, the National Socialist elite had arrived . . . . Hitler turned to the assembled company. Now I saw that his face was purple with agitation and with the heat gathering in the dome. He shouted uncontrollably as I had never seen him do before, as if he was going to burst: 'There will be no mercy now. Anyone who stands in our way will be cut down. The German people will not tolerate leniency. Every Communist official will be shot where he is found. The Communist deputies must he hanged this very night. Everybody in league with the Communists must be arrested. There will no longer by any leniency for Social Democrats either.'

I reported on the results of the first interrogations of Marinus van der Lubbe that in my opinion he was a maniac. Hitler ridiculed my childish view.

From J. Noakes and G. Pridham, *Documents on Nazism*, Jonathan Cape, 1974.

A British view

From *Punch*, 8
March 1933.

THE RED PERIL.

THE OLD CONSUL (*to* HITLER). "THIS IS A HEAVEN-SENT OPPORTUNITY, MY LAD.
IF YOU CAN'T BE A DICTATOR NOW, YOU NEVER WILL BE."

Questions

1 How can you tell that Rudolf Diels was at the scene of the fire very quickly?

2 What might have given Diels the impression that van der Lubbe was 'a maniac'?

3 Was Hitler's reaction to the fire what you would have expected from a head of government? Explain your answer.

4 What evidence can you find in Source A which supports Hitler's version?

5 Does this evidence justify the steps he said he would take? Explain.

6 In the cartoon who is the old consul (Roman ruler)?

7 Explain the significance of the scroll in Hitler's hand.

8 In your own words explain the caption below the cartoon.

9 How valuable to the historian is a cartoon drawn hundreds of miles away from the event it is describing?

27 The March elections, 1933

The Reichstag fire on 27 February gave the Nazis a convenient excuse for silencing all opposition. The very next day Hitler's government issued an emergency decree which took away all civil liberties and gave the police wide powers, as you can see in Source A.

Thus, in the final week of the March election campaign the Nazis were able to ban all Communist Party (KPD) and Social Democratic newspapers, leaflets, meetings and so on. Naturally the Nazis could still use the radio, the post, meeting halls and street demonstrations for their own campaign. The cartoon shows a British view of this situation (Source B). The diary entry (Source C) shows that liberal Germans like Count Kessler were trying to encourage themselves with signs that the Nazis had not won over all the German people. In contrast, any Socialist or KPD councillors at the council meeting in Northeim must have been full of fear and foreboding. Source D is a report of an attack made on them in his first speech by a newly elected Nazi councillor.

A Decree of the Reich President on the Protection of the People and the State, 28 February 1933

Articles 114, 115, 117, 118, 123, 124 and 153 of the constitution of the German Reich are cancelled until further notice. This allows certain restrictions to be imposed on personal freedom, on the right to express a free opinion, the freedom of the press, on association and the right to hold meetings, it allows restrictions on the secrecy of the mail, post and telecommunications systems, the ordering of house searches and confiscation of property and restrictions on property rights.

From the exhibition catalogue, *Questions in German History*, Bonn, 1984.

B 'Voice of the people'

From the *Daily Express*, 4 March 1933.

C Looking for reassurance, 6 March 1933

The Nazis have won 288 seats and 43.9 per cent of the Reichstag vote (as against 196 and 33.1 per cent on 31 July). The Social Democrats, regardless of the scandalous pressure exercised against them and the complete paralysis of their propaganda, have lost only a hundred thousand votes, the KPD only a million. This is astounding and a wonderful tribute to the imperturbability of the 'Marxist Front'. The Nazis and the Nationalists now have constitutionally complete freedom of action for the next four years, though lacking a two-thirds majority to introduce constitutional changes.

From Count Harry Kessler, *The Diaries of a Cosmopolitan* (trans. C. Kessler), Weidenfeld and Nicolson, 1971.

D The Nazi councillor's first speech

We haven t forgotten a single thing. Nor will we hesitate to pay them back for every bit. In the reckoning up it won't be the poor people who were blinded by them, it will be the seducers themselves that we'll settle with, down to the smallest party hack. In locked concentration camps they'll learn how to work for Germany again!

From W. S. Allen, *The Nazi Seizure of Power*, Franklin Watts, 1984.

Questions

1 According to the decree, what things could now be dangerous for individuals or groups to do?

2 In your own words suggest ways in which the government could now interfere in the lives of ordinary people (Source A).

3 What does the British cartoon suggest were the ways in which the Nazis tried to influence the electors in March 1933?

4 This cartoon is a caricature of Hitler and his party. Explain what this means. Can caricatures be of any use to the historian?

5 Does Count Kessler's diary entry suggest that the decree (Source A) was effective? Explain.

6 What reasons might Kessler have had for considering the election results 'a wonderful tribute' to the Social Democrats and the Communists?

7 What difficulty for the Nazis' plans does Kessler say was caused by their getting only 43.9 per cent of the votes?

8 Is Source D the sort of speech you would expect from a new council member? Give reasons for your answer.

9 What does the councillor mean when he describes the Socialist and Communist leaders as 'seducers'?

10 Does the councillor support or contradict the portrayal of the Nazis in the cartoon?

28 The Enabling Act, March 1933

The March elections had not given Hitler the two-thirds majority he needed to change the rules of the constitution so that he could govern Germany as he wished. He was now determined to force the Reichstag, the German Parliament, to get rid of itself.

On 24 March the Reichstag was called to meet in the Kroll Opera House to decide whether to pass the Enabling Act. This would allow Hitler to rule by decree alone for the next four years; there would be no further need for a parliament. Four hundred and forty-one deputies voted for the act, including the Centre Party members who had at first said they would vote against it. Only 94 voted against it. They were all members of the Social Democratic Party (SPD). Their stand against Hitler took a lot of courage, as you can see from the following accounts by men who were in the Kroll Opera House that night. The first (Source A) is the recollection of an SPD deputy; the second (Source B) is that of Kurt Ludecke, a close associate of Hitler's at the time.

A A Social Democrat deputy's view

The wide square in front of the Kroll Opera House was crowded with dark masses of people. We were received with wild choruses: 'We want the Enabling Act!' Youths with swastikas on their chests eyed us insolently, blocked our way, in fact made us run the gauntlet, calling us names like 'Centre pig', 'Marxist sow'. The Kroll Opera House was crawling with armed SA and SS men . . . . When we Social Democrats had taken our seats on the extreme left, SA and SS men lined up at the exits and along the walls behind us in a semicircle. Their expressions boded no good.

Hitler read out his government declaration in a surprisingly calm voice. Only in a few places did he raise it to a fanatical frenzy . . . . Otto Wels [the SPD leader] read out our reply to the government declaration. It was a masterpiece in form and content, a farewell to the fading epoch of human rights and humanity. In concluding, Otto Wels, with his voice half choking, gave our good wishes to the persecuted and oppressed in the country who, though innocent, were already filling the prisons and concentration camps simply on account of their political creed.

This speech made a terrifying impression on all of us . . . .

But Hitler jumped up furiously and launched into a passionate reply . . . .

We tried to damn the flood of Hitler's unjust accusations with interruptions of 'No!', 'An error!', 'False!' But they did us no good. The SA and SS people, who surrounded us in a semicircle along the walls of the hall, hissed loudly and murmured: 'Shut up!', 'Traitors!', 'You'll be strung up today.'

From J. Noakes and G. Pridham, *Documents on Nazism*, Jonathan Cape, 1974.

B A Nazi view: Kurt Ludecke

We were witnessing a dramatic occasion, the best-staged parliamentary play I have ever seen. Yet the outcome was still in doubt. What would the Centrists do? What about the Sozis*?

After a long recess for deliberation, Otto Wels, former paperhanger and the last chairman of the Social Democratic Party, took the platform. He was in an unenviable position, facing a hostile house and surrounded by strong-armed Nazi troopers. Under the circumstances his vote for his party against the bill showed courage.

Speaking monotonously, he protested that his party had never lacked patriotism nor feeling for national honour. He cut a poor figure; his voice seemed the last squeak of a beaten and miserable group. As a critic-spectator at a marvellous play, I was disappointed, and recalled how superbly Hitler had risen to the occasion when, in 1924, he had faced the court a beaten man .... Now he (Hitler) rose briskly for an improvised reply .... If ever a party was annihilated by a speech, it happened then. The house swelled with cheers with roars of laughter, with enthusiasm and derision. And when he ended: 'I do not want your votes! Germany will be free, but not through you!' the storm of applause was a cyclone. One had heard that sort of thing in great mass meetings, but this was a German elite.

From Kurt Ludecke, *I knew Hitler*, Charles Scribner's Sons, 1937.

Social Democrats

Questions

1 Why did the Social Democrats show courage simply in going into the Reichstag meeting?

2 Can you think of any reasons why there were no Communist deputies there?

3 Why do you think Otto Wels was 'half choking' when he was concluding his speech?

4 On what aspects of this meeting are both eye-witnesses agreed?

5 What is it that they give a totally different picture of?

6 Was Kurt Ludecke being fair when he compared Otto Wels' performance in 1933 with Hitler's back in 1924? Think carefully about the different situations they faced and what was disturbing Otto Wels so much.

7 Find out what an 'elite' is and then explain why Kurt Ludecke placed so much stress upon their response to Hitler's speech.

8 Improvise a conversation between two Centre Party members when they get home from the Opera House. One thinks they have done the right thing in voting with Hitler for the Enabling Act and the other thinks they have been fooled.

29 Crushing the opposition, 1933

Soon after Hitler became Chancellor the SA and SS were made auxiliary police. Now they had the power, they were determined to settle old scores and win some prizes. Their main targets were their traditional enemies on the left; the Communists, the Social Democrats and the Trade Unions.

On the afternoon of 9 March 1933 the Volksfreund House, the SPD and Trade Union headquarters in Brunswick in North Germany, was raided by the SA and the SS. Similar raids took place across the country. We know about them because they were reported to Social Democrats who had fled from Germany and were keeping the party going in exile. Source A is part of one report sent to them which was compiled by eye-witnesses.

While the trade-union leaders were hoping that Hitler's new government would go no further, Hitler caught them unawares. May Day was declared a national holiday. Early the next day trade union offices across Germany were occupied (Source B). Their officials were arrested, beaten and thrown into concentration camps.

A The raid on the Volksfreund House

There, lorries with SA and SS had driven up at 4.05 p.m. The porter promptly closed the doors. But the Nazis broke the big display windows and pushed into the building through the holes. They opened fire inside the building with a number of rifles and revolvers. During this, the 28-year-old salesman, Hans Saile, was killed by a shot in the stomach . . . .

The intruders rushed up the stairs and smashed in the locked doors with their rifle butts. Union secretaries, employees, typists, Co-op salesgirls were all driven together with cudgels, rifles, revolvers and daggers. Then, with the order 'Hands up!', they were locked up for hours, before being released with kicks and slaps . . . .

The former police lieutenant, Richard Neuenfeldt, now a driver with the Volksfreund . . . was busy doing car repairs in the yard at the onset of the occupation. He was recognised and beaten on his head and face with cudgels, steel pipes, revolver butts and metal tools until he collapsed unconscious. Even then he was kicked, dragged across the yard and thrown out. Neuenfeldt is an ex-serviceman, who served at the front and fought right through the war. Those who beat him up – a typical case that was repeated countless times – were 20-year-old boys. As a result of this beating up, Neuenfeldt is a broken man, physically and mentally.

During the course of the action, the private tenants of the Volksfreund building were raided in their flats, abused, threatened with weapons and beaten . . . .

The regular police had meanwhile blocked off the surrounding streets with a strong force. The Nazis looted the building in front of their very eyes.

From J. Noakes and G. Pridham, *Documents of Nazism*, Jonathan Cape, 1974.

Immediately after the raid on the building, Comrade Dr Heinrich Jasper, the former Minister-President of Brunswick, rang up the Police-President .... He accused the solicitor and deputy, Alpers, leader of the SS in Brunswick, of armed riot, unlawful assembly, house-breaking and disturbance of public order ....

There was of course no redress. On the contrary, Alpers became Minister of Justice (in Brunswick) under the Hitler regime.

B SA troops occupy the Trade Union Headquarters in Berlin, 2 May 1933

Questions

1 Estimate how many Nazis took part in this raid.

2 How was it clear from the start that they were in deadly earnest?

3 Think about the kind of people who were in the building. What kind of resistance could they have been expected to put up?

4 Why did the SA and SS pick on Richard Neuenfeldt especially?

5 What does this report suggest about the kind of young men who took part in this raid?

6 How does your answer to question 5 explain the special appeal of these squads to certain young men at the time?

7 Would you expect Dr Jasper's complaint to have been taken seriously at this time? Explain your answer.

8 How does Source B give a very different impression of the government's treatment of the trade unions?

9 Suggest reasons why the scene in the photograph is so peaceful.

30 Night of the Long Knives, 1934

By the summer of 1934 Hitler had decided that the SA, led by his old friend, Ernst Roehm, was becoming a dangerous liability. Roehm was said to want to unite the SA and the regular army under his command. The Reichswehr would not stand for this and Hitler was not prepared to risk turning the army against him when it was the only organisation left which was capable of removing him.

All the SA leaders including Roehm were summoned to a place near Munich for a meeting. Goering was left behind in Berlin to deal with the SA there, and Hitler and Goebbels flew down to Munich to catch Roehm and the others unawares at their hotel in the middle of the night. After the war Hitler's chauffeur, Kempka, and the local prison governor described what happened on the 'Night of the Long Knives' (Source A) and the day after (Source B).

Source C is a famous British cartoon of the time by David Low. Source D is an entry in the diary of William Shirer, an American journalist.

A Hitler's chauffeur describes the night

As soon as I have turned the car so that it is ready to leave in a moment, I rush into the hotel with my gun at ready. In the hall I meet Uhl, the leader of Roehm's staff guard. Schreck is taking him at gunpoint down to the laundry room which for the next hour serves as the first prison for the arrested SA leaders . . . .

I run quickly up the stairs to the first floor where Hitler is just coming out of Roehm's bedroom . . . . Roehm comes out of his room in a blue suit and with a cigar in the corner of his mouth. Hitler glares at him but says nothing. Two detectives take Roehm to the vestibule of the hotel where he throws himself into an armchair and orders coffee from the waiter . . . .

Meanwhile, upstairs in the corridor things are getting quite lively. SA leaders are coming out of their rooms and being arrested. Hitler shouts at each one: 'Have you had anything to do with Roehm's schemes?' Naturally, they all deny it, but that doesn't help them in the least. Hitler usually knows about the individual; occasionally, he asks Goebbels or Lutze a question. And then comes the decision: 'Arrested!'

From J. Noakes and G. Pridham, Documents of Nazism, Jonathan Cape, 1974.

B The governor describes the morning after

Next morning two SS men asked at the reception desk to be taken to Roehm . . . . It took hours of telephoning to check their papers . . . . When at last it became clear that they had an order from Hitler, the two murderers had to be taken to Roehm in the new building.

There they handed over a Browning to Roehm, who once again asked to speak to Hitler. They ordered him to shoot himself . . . . When the time was up, the two SS men re-entered the cell, and found Roehm standing with his chest bared. Immediately, one of them from the door shot him in the throat, and Roehm collapsed on the floor.

From J. Noakes and G. Pridham, Documents of Nazism, Jonathan Cape, 1974.

C 'They salute with both hands now'

THEY SALUTE WITH BOTH HANDS NOW.

From the *Evening Standard*, 3 July 1934.

D Hitler blames Roehm

Hitler faced his SA storm troopers today for the first time since the bloody purge. In a harangue to fifty thousand of them he 'absolved' them from blame for the Roehm 'revolt'. There was considerable tension in the stadium and I noticed Hitler's own SS bodyguard was drawn up in force in front of him, separating him from the mass of the brownshirts. We wondered if just one of those fifty thousand brownshirts wouldn't pull a revolver, but not one did.

From William L. Shirer, *Berlin Diary 1934–41*, Sphere, 1970.

Questions

1. How can you tell that Hitler's chauffeur was expecting trouble?

2. What impression does Roehm seem to be trying to create on the night of his arrest?

3. How important a part does the chauffeur suggest Hitler played in this night of arrests?

4. Bearing in mind your answer to question 3, is the cartoonist's portrayal of Hitler correct? Explain.

5. How are Goering and Goebbels caricatured in the cartoon?

6. Why did the 'murderers' in Source B bother to try to get Roehm to kill himself? Was his refusal cowardice? Explain.

7. Why do you think Roehm asked to speak to Hitler?

8. What do Sources A and D suggest were the 'official' reasons given for the Roehm purge?

Part 7

The Nazi state

31 The Nazi state and the workers

One of the first tasks of Hitler's government was to create jobs for Germany's six million unemployed. Money was poured into building roads, hospitals, schools and so on. Much of the work was done by labour service gangs drawn from the unemployed. Others found work in arms factories when Germany began re-arming and in the forces when conscription was reintroduced.

However, job creation went alongside the Nazi determination to control the entire labour force. Trade unions were smashed and all workers were forced to join the Nazi Labour Front.

Source A is the proclamation by the Labour Front Leader, Robert Ley, in May 1933. Source B gives one impression of a labour service gang, from the daily notes of Nora Waln, an American journalist living in Germany in 1933. Source C gives a different picture. A Munich police report of 1935 suggests that complaints among workers were widespread (Source D).

A Ley's proclamation to the workers

German workers and employees! ... Three months of National Socialist Government have already proved to you: Adolf Hitler is your friend! Adolf Hitler struggles for your liberty! Adolf Hitler gives you bread! ... We will not let you alone until you give us your entire and genuine support .... For we know that without the German worker there is no German nation .... It is not as if we wanted to disrupt and destroy the unions .... No, workers! Your institutions are sacred to us .... I swear to you we shall not only preserve everything which exists, we shall build up even further the protection of workers' rights ....

Workers and peasants on a broad front, together with the professions and skilled labour – Forward with Hitler for Germany!

From J. Noakes and G. Pridham, *Documents of Nazism*, Jonathan Cape, 1974.

B Labour service gangs: a journalist's view

In double file they passed down the village street. Thirty-two young men, near six feet tall and handsomely built; stripped to the waist, their smooth skins reddened by sun and wind; trousered in grey-green cotton cloth freshly laundered; booted to the knees in stout leather .... Thus the first German Labour Corps I saw went by, their eyes glancing neither to the right nor to the left.

'Heil! Heil!' cheered the villagers.

From Nora Waln, *Reaching for the Stars*, Little, Brown, 1939.

Labour service gangs in action

Labour service gangs: a police view

For the most part the workers complain about insufficient wages. They do not satisfy the needs of food, clothing and accommodation ... investigations have established that the same poor mood arising from the same mentality is to be encountered among most workers on the other construction sites.

From Ian Kershaw, *Popular Opinion and Political Dissent in the Third Reich*, Clarendon Press, 1983.

Questions

1 What are the blatant propaganda statements in Ley's proclamation?

2 After looking back to Unit 29, describe the blatant lie told here by Ley.

3 If you didn't know the men in Source B were workers what would you think they were? Is this likeness accidental? Explain.

4 Why do you think the villagers cheered them?

5 What is the basic complaint of the workers in Source D?

6 If this 'poor mood' was common, why do we hear so little about it?

7 What might be proved from the fact that the police made regular reports like the one in Source D?

8 What caption would a writer such as Nora Waln have given to the photograph?

9 Does Source D suggest that Ley fulfilled his promises?

32 The Nazi state and women

Hitler had very conservative views on women. He believed they were inferior to men and should be submissive and obedient to them. These attitudes are made clear from a speech Hitler gave to the Nazi Women's League in 1934 (Source A).

The Nazis put tremendous pressure on women to give up their jobs, get married and have large families. Mothers were honoured publicly, as the Nazi newspaper (Source B) shows. They were awarded a bronze cross for four children, a silver cross for six, and a gold for eight. Source D shows how anti-Nazi cartoonists portrayed such mothers.

Women who were sterile could be divorced with ease. Advertisements like the one in Source C became commonplace. Not everyone agreed. In 1934 a few women were daring enough to publish a challenge to Hitler's views (Source E).

A Hitler explains their role to Nazi women

If the man's world is said to be the State ... then it may perhaps be said that the woman's is a smaller world. For her world is her husband, her family, her children, and her home. But what would become of the greater world if there were no one to tend and care for the smaller one? . . .

We do not consider it correct for the women to interfere in the world of the man .... We consider it natural if these two worlds remain distinct. To the one belongs the strength of feeling, the strength of the soul. To the other belongs the strength of vision, of toughness, of decision, and of the willingness to act ....

... the programme of our National Socialist Women's movement has in reality but one single point, and that point is the child.

From J. Noakes and G. Pridham, *Documents of Nazism*, Jonathan Cape, 1974.

B Honouring the mothers

In August 1939 3 million German mothers will be honoured; in future all members of the party's youth organisations will be duty-bound to salute wearers of the Mother's Honour Cross and thus the young generation will be paying homage to them.

From R. Grunberger, *A Social History of the Third Reich*, Penguin, 1974.

C Wife and mother wanted

Aryan doctor ... desires male progeny* through a registry office marriage with a healthy aryan, virginal, young, unassuming, economy-minded woman, adapted to hard work, broad-hipped, flat-heeled and earringless.

From R. Grunberger, *A Social History of the Third Reich*, Penguin, 1974.

* *children*

Introducing Frau Mueller

'And now I will introduce Frau Mueller, who, up to now, has brought 12 children into the world!'

E Some women complain to Hitler

Today, man is being educated not for, but against, marriage. Men are grouped together in clubs and hostels .... Woman stays back further and further in the shadow of loneliness .... We see our daughters growing up in stupid aimlessness living only in the vague hope of perhaps getting a man and having children .... A son, even the youngest, today laughs in his mother's face. He regards her as his natural servant, and women in general as merely willing tools of his aims.

From R. Grunberger, *A Social History of the Third Reich*, Penguin, 1974.

Questions

1 What should be a woman's chief responsibilities, according to Hitler?

2 In which ways do you think Hitler's views about women matched his political ideas?

3 What do you think of the suggestion in Source B?

4 How does the cartoon mock and ridicule the Nazis?

5 What does the newspaper advertisement tell us about this particular man's attitude towards women?

6 Would you reply, if female, to such an advertisement? If male, would you advertise in this way? Explain your answer.

7 Do you think the women who wrote to Hitler in their book (Source E) were right to be worried about any of the trends they describe? Give reasons for your answer.

8 All the sources mention children. Why do you think children were so important to the Nazis?

33 The Nazi state and young people

In Hitler's Germany all the old loyalties to one's parents, friends, school and God were to be replaced by just one loyalty – to 'The Leader' or 'Der Fuehrer'. Young people were organised into groups which would teach them this; the Hitler Youth for boys and the League of German Maidens for girls. On 1 March 1933 Melita Maschmann secretly joined the girls' section of the League of German Maidens. Her parents had taken her to see a Nazi victory parade on the night Hitler was made Chancellor and in her autobiography, written after the war (Source A), she explains the special appeal of the Nazis to young people, the activities of her local group, and how her schoolwork was soon affected.

Compare the girls' activities with those for boys in the Hitler Youth. The appeal of camp life comes out in the page from a child's colouring book (Source B). Boys at these camps spent most of their time doing physical training and having political lessons, in which slogans and poems like those in Sources C and D were learned by heart.

A German Maidens

On the evening of January 30th [1933] my parents took us children, my twin brother and myself, into the centre of the city. There we witnessed the torchlight procession with which the National Socialists celebrated their victory. Some of the uncanny feel of that night remains with me even today. The crashing tread of the feet, the sombre pomp of the red and black flags, the flickering light from the torches on the faces and the songs . . . .

For hours the columns marched by. Again and again amongst them we saw groups of boys and girls scarcely older than ourselves . . . .

'For the flag we are ready to die', the torch-bearers had sung. It was not a matter of clothing or food or school essays, but of life and death.

The time was passed in paying subscriptions, drawing up countless lists and swotting up the words of songs . . . . Discussions on political texts from, say, *Mein Kampf*, quickly ended in silence . . . .

I remember with more pleasure the weekend outings, the hikes, sports, campfires and youth hostelling. Occasionally, there would be field exercises with neighbouring groups. If there was any rivalry between them the game often degenerated into a first class brawl.

In the Upper Second Class I began frequently to play truant from school. Work for the Hitler Youth took up more and more of my time and energy. I would often leave the house at 5 in the morning and only arrive at school for the second or third lesson . . . . Every unit wanted to have the best group 'home', the most interesting log, the biggest collection for the Winter Relief Fund, and so forth.'

From M. Maschmann, *Account Rendered* (trans. G. Strachen), Abelard-Schuman, 1964.

B Hitler Youth at camp

C Hitler Youth slogans

'Tough as leather, swift as grey hounds,
hard as Krupps* steel.'
'Germany must live, even if we have to die!'

From M. Maschmann,
Account Rendered (trans.
G. Strachen), Abelard
and Schuman, 1964.

* *a leading steel firm*

D Hitler Youth Poem, 1941

You, Fuehrer, are our commander!
We stand in your name.
The Reich is the object of our struggle,
It is the beginning and the Amen.

Your word is the heartbeat of our deeds;
Your faith builds cathedrals for us.
And even when death reaps the last harvest
The crown of the Reich never falls.

From J. Noakes and G. Pridham, *Documents of Nazism*, Jonathan Cape, 1974.

Questions

1 What impressed Melita Maschmann so much about the marchers in Source A?

2 What seems to have made her want to join them?

3 Can you understand her response? Explain your answer.

4 Did life as a member live up to her expectations? Give an example to explain your answer.

5 What was the effect of joining the Hitler Youth on her school work?

6 What drove the children on from one activity to another, according to Melita Maschmann? Can you imagine you and your friends being like this?

7 How was the government trying to make camp life look attractive in the colouring book?

8 What values do the Hitler Youth slogans in Source C stress? Are these admirable qualities?

9 What is the point of getting young people to memorise slogans and poems like these?

10 Apart from Hitler, what else does the poem suggest young people should care about most? For what part of Nazi thinking is this meant to prepare young people?

34 The Nazi state and education

Adolf Hitler was a fanatic who wanted far more than simple political power. He wanted to mould the German people into an army that would believe what it was told and be ready to fight and die for those beliefs. The extract from Mein Kampf *(Source A) makes it plain that the classroom was the place where the future citizens of the Reich were to be shaped.*

This could be done by learning poems like the one in Source B or studying books which glorified war. Source C is taken from a book written for fourteen-year-olds on the German victory over the Russians at the battle of Tannenburg in 1914. Teachers were forced to join the Nazi Teachers' Association. The post-war interview with a teacher (Source D) shows the great pressure to teach in the Nazi way. The photograph of kindergarten children giving the Nazi salute shows that indoctrination began before school age.

Mein Kampf – Hitler on education

Our admiration of every great deed must be bathed in pride that its fortunate performer is a member of our own people. From all the innumerable great names of German history, the greatest must be picked out and introduced to the youth so persistently that they become pillars of an unshakeable sentiment.

The curriculum must be systematically built up along these lines so that when the young man leaves his school he is not a half pacifist, democrat, or something else, but a whole German.

. . . beginning in youth one iron principle must be hammered into those heads which are still capable of education: any man who loves his people proves it solely by the sacrifices which he is prepared to make for it . . . .

. . . then a people of citizens will some day arise, bound to one another and forged together by a common love and a common pride, unshakeable and invincible forever . . . .

The crown of the folkish* state's entire work of education and training must be to burn the racial sense and racial feeling into the instinct and the intellect, the heart and brain of the youth entrusted to it. No boy and no girl must leave school without having been led to an ultimate realisation of the necessity and essence of blood purity.

From Adolf Hitler, *Mein Kampf* (trans. R. Manheim), Hutchinson, 1974.

* *belonging to German people or race*

A poem for the classroom

You must believe in Germany as firmly, clearly and
truly as you believe in the sun, the moon, and the starlight.
You must believe in Germany, as if Germany were yourself;
and as you believe your soul strikes towards eternity.
You must believe in Germany – or your life is but death.
And you must fight for Germany until the new dawn comes.

From M. Maschmann, *Account Rendered* (trans. G. Strachen), Abelard-Schuman, 1964.

C   Glorifying war

A Russian soldier tried to bar the infiltrator's way, but Otto's bayonet slid gratingly between the Russian's ribs, so that he collapsed groaning. There it lay before him, simple and distinguished, his dream's desire, the Iron Cross.

From W. S. Allen, *The Nazi Seizure of Power*, Franklin Watts, 1984.

D   Indoctrinating teachers

You had to go to the indoctrination sessions constantly and these ideas were drummed into you. And you had to learn them because you had to be very careful about what you said.

From R. Grunberger, *A Social History of the Third Reich*, Penguin, 1974.

E   Indoctrinating the toddlers

Questions

1 What is the chief aim of education, according to Hitler in *Mein Kampf*?

2 Use Source A to illustrate why history and biology became the two most important subjects in Nazi schools.

3 Why do you think Hitler includes girls in his last comment in Source A when he hasn't bothered to mention them elsewhere?

4 Is Source B an example of censorship, propaganda or indoctrination? Explain your answer.

5 Children had to learn this poem off by heart. Which parts of it do you think pupils of your age would understand?

6 What do you imagine happened at 'indoctrination sessions'?

7 What does the fact that indoctrination sessions had to be held tell us?

8 Why did teachers have to be careful what they said, especially in the classroom?

9 Why did the Nazi Party take the involvement of youngsters like those in the photograph so seriously?

10 What do you think the 'Hitler Salute' meant to these children?

35   The Nazi state and the churches

Hitler's desire to mould the German people into a national community loyal only to him created a difficulty for Christians, who taught that the first duty was to God and one's conscience. At first Hitler bought the co-operation of the churches by promising to protect their rights. Sources A and B show how the Catholic bishops and the Catholic Schoolteachers' Association explained the position shortly after Hitler came to power.

The Catholic Church's first outspoken attack on Nazism came in 1941 when the government started a programme of killing mentally ill and handicapped people. Source D is an extract from a sermon given by the Catholic Archbishop of Muenster on 3 August 1941. The death programme was then officially dropped but not before some 60,000–80,000 sick and handicapped people had been murdered by gassing or injection.

Hitler tried to control the Protestant Christians by creating a Nazi Church, the 'German Christians'. Some Protestants refused to have anything to do with it, and individuals like Pastor Niemoeller were sent to concentration camps for their opposition. But, on the whole, the Protestant and Catholic Churches seemed to ignore the evils of Nazism. Source C shows how Hitler's Churchmen were the target of much anti-Nazi criticism.

A   Pronouncement of Catholic Bishops

Catholic Christians, for whom the opinion of their Church is sacred, need no particular admonition* to be loyal to the legally constituted authorities, to fulfil their civic duties conscientiously, and to reject absolutely any illegal or revolutionary activity . . . .

. . . they should avoid in church and at church functions, out of respect for their sacredness, anything which might be construed as a party political demonstration.

Encourage . . . the Catholic Associations whose work is so full of blessings for church, nation and Fatherland, for Christian culture and social peace.

From J. Noakes and G. Pridham, *Documents on Nazism*, Jonathan Cape, 1974.

* *strong advice*

B   The Catholic Teachers' Association

Now the whole German nation in all its various parts, including the Catholics, has been summoned to cooperate and to build a new order. We must – and here we completely agree with the leader of the national movement – we must first become an internally unified nation of German men and women. We must put aside everything which divides us . . . in order once more to become a nation which believes in honour, cleanliness, and loyalty.

From J. Noakes and G. Pridham, *Documents on Nazism*, Jonathan Cape, 1974.

Anti-Nazi propaganda poster: the German United
Church

„Wir treten zum Beten".

'We go forward to pray.'

D August 1941 – Bishop Galen attacks murder

Catholic Christians!

For several months we have been hearing reports that patients in clinics and nursing homes for the mentally ill, who have been ill for some time and may seem incurable, are being forcibly removed on orders from Berlin. Then usually, after a short time, the relatives receive notification that the patient has died, that the corpse has been burnt and that the ashes can be delivered. There is a general suspicion, bordering on certainty, that these numerous unexpected deaths of mental patients do not occur of themselves but are deliberately induced . . . .

In the face of this, the German Bishops declare: Never, and under no circumstances, must a human being kill an innocent human being apart from war and justified self-defence . . . .

Once it is admitted that people have the right to kill unproductive beings even if it now affects only poor, defenceless, mentally sick persons, then a principle will have been established which will license the murder of all unproductive people.

From J. Noakes and G. Pridham, *Documents on Nazism*, Jonathan Cape, 1974.

Questions

1 Does Source A suggest that Hitler would be pleased with the arrangement he had made with the Catholic Church?

2 If the second instruction had been ignored how might opposition from an organisation like the Catholic Church have affected Hitler's position?

3 Which Nazi beliefs or practices were completely at odds with 'Christian culture and social peace'?

4 Who is 'the leader of the national movement' in Source B?

5 In your own words say why the Catholic teachers believed they should help to build Hitler's 'New Order'.

6 Imagine a Catholic teacher who had doubts about the Association's pronouncement. What would most worry him or her as (a) a Christian, (b) a teacher?

7 Why did Bishop Galen's sermon (Source D) take such courage?

8 Was the Bishop able to prove his allegations? Explain.

9 What do the difficulties of proof tell you about the problems of opposition inside a totalitarian regime?

10 On what grounds does the Bishop attack the killing of the mentally sick?

11 How does the cartoon condemn the Nazi Christian Church?

12 Do you think it is an effective cartoon? Explain.

36 The Nazi state and Jewish people

The 1930s were a nightmare time for Germans who were Jews. They were hounded from their jobs, businesses and homes. They were banned from social clubs, schools, cinemas, theatres, swimming pools and parks. Anti-semitism had always been part of the Nazi programme, and was backed up by streams of crude propaganda. Source A is an example from the 1932 election campaign and Source B is from the British Daily Herald in 1933 describing how a propaganda film was made.

The most vicious portrayals of Jews, which were often pornographic, appeared in the Nazi paper Der Sturmer, edited by Julius Streicher. Source C is an account by an Australian professor of history who visited Germany in 1937 and saw boys at a youth camp reading Streicher's paper. He also commented on the general attitude of the Germans towards persecution of the Jews. In Source D, Melita Maschmann tried to explain, in 1964, her attitude to Jews when she was a loyal member of the League of German Maidens (see Unit 33).

Nazi election poster, 1932

'Freed from misery, freed from Jews'

B The making of a propaganda film

The chief scene photographed on August 11th was a route march of storm detachments led by Horst Wessel. Bearded Jews and persons of pronouncedly Jewish appearance were chosen for preference, two Rabbis among them.

The Jews were made to climb by means of a ladder on to the roofs of low houses, and, as the Nazi Procession went by, to shout, 'Perish the Nazis', 'Death to Fascism', 'Red Front'* or 'Hail Moscow' with the proper gestures. The Jews were also given pieces of cork to simulate stones, and had to throw these at the marchers. The rehearsing and photography lasted in all about three hours.

From the *Daily Herald*, 2 September 1933.

**The Communist cry*

C Professor Roberts on 'Der Sturmer', 1937

One of the most painful sights I saw in Germany was at a boys' camp . . . after a display of staggeringly efficient physical exercises they were dismissed and crowded to the Sturmer-stall to get the last issue of Streicher's paper. Young boys gazed at the cartoons in rapt admiration; and, when I asked a Black Guard officer with me whether he did not see anything funny in the grotesqueries of 'Der Sturmer', he replied: 'It is not funny. They must be taught the truth about the Jews.' . . . I looked back at the growing groups round the newspapers and then at a cartoon in my hand showing a Jew disembowelling a beautiful German girl.

The traveller in Germany is impressed by the general consensus of opinion that such persecution (of Jews) is a good thing. I had expected many people to argue that it was an unwelcome necessity, forced on them by propaganda or by the pressure of events, but this was not the case . . . . I met nobody in Germany who adopted an apologetic attitude.

From S. H. Roberts, *The House that Hitler Built*, Methuen, 1937.

D An imaginary letter to an old Jewish friend

Rosa Cohn was a Jewish classmate of ours, but I did not really connect her with 'The Jews' . . . . In preaching that all the misery of the nation was due to the Jews or that the Jewish spirit was seditious* and Jewish blood corrupting, I was not compelled to think of you or old Herr Lewy [a neighbour] or Rosa Cohn: I thought only of the bogey-man 'The Jew'. And when I heard that the Jews were being driven from their professions and homes and imprisoned in ghettos, the points switched automatically in my mind to steer me round the thought that such a fate could also overtake you or old Lewy. It was only 'the Jew' who has being persecuted and 'made harmless'.

From M. Maschmann, *Account Rendered* (trans. G. Strachen), Abelard-Schuman, 1964.

* *treasonable*

Questions

1 How does the poster caricature Jewish people?

2 What is the propaganda message about Jewish people?

3 What contrast is being deliberately drawn between the Jewish man and the group on the left?

4 Why did the film makers seek persons of 'pronouncedly Jewish appearance' for the film in Source B?

5 How does the film present Jews as a very dangerous group?

6 Why, do you think, did the Jewish people take part in this film?

7 How do Sources A and B illustrate what 'propaganda' is?

8 What kind of organisation was probably running the boys' camp in Source C?

9 What struck Professor Roberts as so 'painful' about the boys he saw?

10 What can you learn about Germany in 1937 from the fact that Professor Roberts expected no more criticism of the persecution of the Jews than calling it an 'unwelcome necessity'?

11 Melita Maschmann touches upon the point that is at the bottom of all racist attitudes; what is it?

12 Write an imaginary reply to Melita Maschmann's letter from her old Jewish friend.

37 'Crystal Night', November 1938

The full savagery of Nazi anti-Jewish terror may not have been fully understood by ordinary Germans until 'Crystal Night' in 1938 when the SA and the SS went on an orgy of destruction. Synagogues, Jewish houses and shops were destroyed throughout Germany. Goebbels, the Propaganda Minister, explained it as a 'spontaneous' outburst by the German people as a whole after the killing of a Nazi official in Paris by a young Jewish boy. The American Consul's report of what happened in Leipzig gives a different version of who was involved (Source A). Melita Maschmann later tried to analyse why loyal Nazis like herself reacted in the way they did (Source B). There is no doubt that the terror of that night stunned most Germans. Their general response seems to have been to stay at home and say nothing about it but this was not always the case. A Jewish emigrant remembers how much help Jews were given in Munich at that time (Source C).

A Crystal Night in Leipzig

At 3 am on 10 November 1938 was unleashed a barrage of Nazi ferocity as had no equal hitherto in Germany, or very likely anywhere else in the world since savagery began. Jewish buildings were smashed into and contents demolished or looted. In one of the Jewish sections an 18 year-old boy was hurled from a three-storey window to land with both legs broken on a street littered with burning beds and other household furniture and effects from his family's and other apartments ...

Jewish shop windows by the hundreds were systematically and wantonly smashed throughout the entire city ... many of the shop windows at the time of the demolition were filled with costly furs that were seized before the windows could be boarded up ....

Three synagogues in Leipzig were fired simultaneously by incendiary bombs and all sacred objects and records desecrated or destroyed, in most cases hurled through the windows and burned in the streets. No attempts whatsoever were made to quench the fires ...

Ferocious as was the violation of property, the most hideous phase of the so-called 'spontaneous' action has been the wholesale arrest and transportation to concentration camps of male German Jews between the ages of 16 and 60 .... Having demolished buildings and hurled most of the movable effects on to the streets, the insatiably sadistic perpetrators threw many of the trembling inmates into a small stream that flows through the Zoological Park, commanding horrified spectators to spit at them, defile them with mud and jeer at their plight .... The slightest manifestation of sympathy evoked a positive fury on the part of the perpetrators, and the crowd was powerless to do anything but turn horror-stricken eyes from the scene of abuse, or leave the vicinity. These tactics were carried out the entire morning of 10 November without police intervention and they applied to men, women and children.

From J. Noakes and G. Pridham, *Documents on Nazism*, Jonathan Cape, 1974.

A young Nazi's reaction

I said to myself: the Jews are the enemies of the New Germany. Last night they had a taste of what this means. Let us hope that World Jewry, which has resolved to hinder Germany's 'New steps towards greatness', will take the events of last night as a warning. If the Jew sows hatred against us all over the world, they must learn that we have hostages for them in our own hands.

From M. Maschmann *Account Rendered* (trans. G. Strachen), Abelard-Schuman, 1964.

A Jewish survivor honours his protectors

The mood among the Christian population in Munich is wholly against the action. I encountered the most expressive sympathy and compassion from all sides. It had been generally presumed that the houses would be attacked on the Friday evening [11 November]. Aryan people from the area, unknown to me, offered to accommodate my family for the night. Despite the ban on sales to Jews, grocers asked Jews whether they needed anything, bakers delivered bread irrespective of the ban etc. All Christians behaved impeccably.

From Ian Kershaw, *Popular Opinion and Political Dissent in the Third Reich*, Clarendon Press, 1983.

Questions

1 Find two pieces of evidence in Source A that deny Goebbels' statement that the violence was 'spontaneous'.

2 Does the American Consul's report suggest that the acts of violence were isolated and minor? Explain.

3 What most disturbed and horrified the American Consul?

4 Does Source A give any evidence that the violence had official backing?

5 Use the American Consul's report to show how ordinary people reacted. Is this what you would expect? Explain.

6 What propaganda lies did Melita Maschmann accept as truth in Source B?

7 How do you explain the different response described in Source C?

8 Look at the sources on the churches in Unit 35. What different impression about Christian attitudes to Nazism do they give? Can you explain the difference?

9 Write a continuation of the Jewish emigrant's letter (Source C) explaining why he and his family have finally decided to leave Germany for good. Use Sources A and B to make your letter contain authentic detail.

38 The Nazi terror machine

By the end of Hitler's first year in power a system of terror had been created. The SA, SS and Gestapo (Secret State Police) enforced Hitler's will with blind obedience and utter ruthlessness. Old factories like one at Dachau, near Munich, were converted into concentration camps for 'trouble makers' such as trade unionists, Communists, Social Democrats, homosexuals, gypsies and, of course, Jews.

Rumours of cold-blooded torture in these places spread like wildfire, helping to increase the atmosphere of fear and suspicion. Nora Waln, an American journalist who was living in Germany at the time, kept notes of what she saw and heard (Source A). These were written up into a book in 1937.

Count Kessler, a liberal critic of Hitler's regime, had been warned during a trip abroad not to return to Germany and had settled in Paris as a refugee. In his diary (Source B) he wrote down what other refugees fleeing from Hitler told him.

Kurt Ludecke had been one of Hitler's closest advisers in the 1920s, but, after a disagreement with Hitler, Ludecke became a political prisoner in one of the early concentration camps. After his escape, he fled to the United States, where in 1937 he wrote an account of his experiences (Source C).

A   An American in Germany

(In a restaurant)
'Hush, speak through a flower!' It seemed a curious answer. Because I look puzzled, it was amplified: 'Do not speak the names of government officials or party members unless you praise them.'

From Nora Waln, *Reaching for the Stars*, Little, Brown, 1939.

(Later that day)
I was hushed and not answered until we were in our host's house. Then, after the servant had left the room, pillows were put down along the crack of the door, a wad of plasticine stuck in the keyhole, and the telephone – which in Germany plugs into a wall socket – pulled from its connection.

B   The Paris diary of a German exile

Paris, Tuesday, 25th April 1933
The Nazis are continuing to arrest and maltreat working people in a dreadful manner. They abduct a man from his home, keep him for a week to a fortnight, thrash him over and over again, and constantly threaten him with death. When he returns home, he is a physical and mental wreck.

From Count Harry Kessler, *The Diaries of a Cosmopolitan* (trans. C. Kessler), Weidenfeld and Nicolson, 1971.

Paris, Wednesday, 24th May 1933
But what gets the victims down more than anything, said Helmer [a German refugee], is that they are forced to watch the ill-usage of their fellows. That induces complete breakdown.

A Nazi suffers in a concentration camp

The whole thing [his arrest] was so incredible that I did not come to myself for days . . . we were routed at 4.15 in the morning, and it went hard with the man who did not instantly leap to his feet . . . .

After bed-making, we all stood aimlessly about until roll call at seven in the courtyard, followed by morning drill to put us in shape . . . . Among us were men old and ill, men who had never practised knee-bending with backside on heels and arms stretched out! . . .

The nights were most to be dreaded, with the smell of closely herded men hanging dense under the ceiling. Then I would feel that I must get out of this soon or go to pieces . . . .

At any hour of the twenty-four, we would hear yellings and stumblings on the stairs, or the fearful cries and gasps of beaten men, until their moans were stifled in the bunker, below. . . .

One night the screaming and groaning went on till morning. Some thirty men had been arrested as arson suspects in a village near by. I saw some of them being carried away with swollen heads and bruised bodies. After six weeks of hell, all of them were dismissed; they had all been innocent . . . .

In the bunker, when prisoners were fed after days of starving, I saw horrible sights. I saw the familiar face of Neubauer, the Communist deputy; he had been there since the day I was first ordered before the Kommandant. They had flogged him on the back with cow hides soaked in water, but he had not broken down . . . .

One day a transport of over a hundred cripples and invalids arrived . . . [among them] lay weeping a little man, sixty-seven years old, broken by life. He was a country doctor, unpolitical and harmless. But he did not like the Nazis, and he had committed the crime of deleting a Nazi election slogan which had been smeared on his own fence.

Looking at him, I felt ashamed to be a Nazi.

From Kurt Ludecke, *I knew Hitler*, Charles Scribner's Sons, 1937.

Questions

1 Why did Nora Waln's friends feel the need to take precautions?

2 Were Kessler's diary entries opinion, fact or rumour? How did you decide?

3 How do the dates of his entries provide a clue to the Nazis' success in dealing with any opposition?

4 Why, do you think, it was watching the 'ill-usage of their fellows' that made the victims break down?

5 Which part of Source C corroborates Count Kessler's comments?

6 What did Kurt Ludecke find most difficult to bear and why?

7 What might account for the inhuman treatment of Neubauer?

39 Resistance to Hitler

In Berlin there is a building which used to be the Ploetsensee prison. A small red brick outhouse within it was used as an execution chamber until 1945. On this one spot, some 2,500 men, women and adolescents, Germans and non-Germans, were guillotined or hanged. Resistance to Hitler took enormous courage.

In the first months of his exile in Paris, Count Kessler was hopeful about the chances of a rising against the Nazis, as his diary shows (Source A). But as the experience of one German town (Northeim) shows, most people dared not consider resistance (Source B). Yet, resistance groups were constantly at work despite the success of the Gestapo in tracking them down. The most famous was led by von Stauffenberg, an official at the war ministry. At 12.42 pm on 20 July 1944 the bomb he placed in the conference room at Hitler's headquarters exploded. Incredibly, Hitler was only slightly injured. One of the members of the resistance group, who was also a war ministry official, later described that day (Source C).

A Rumours of resistance, 1933

... a revolt among the preponderant part of the German nation – Socialists, Communists, Conservatives, farmers, Catholics, Protestants, industrialists, and the merchant communities of the Hansa cities – which Hitler will be unable to handle. So far the Communists have proved the most active element .... But the others will also be galvanized into greater self-defence. And once the first spark of revolt has been struck, the whole ramshackle Hitler structure will go up in flames.

From Count Harry Kessler, *The Diaries of a Cosmopolitan* (trans. C. Kessler), Weidenfeid and Nicolson, 1971.

B Reasons for not resisting, the late 1930s

Leader of the Reichsbanner
We told them [the SPD members] that every man would have to follow his own conscience now ... when we no longer had the strength to protect them, we could no longer ask them to remain loyal.

From W. S. Allen, *The Nazi Seizure of Power*, Franklin Watts, 1984.

Leader of the Social Democratic Party – advice to members
Join the [Nazi] party. Think of your family.
There's nothing to be gained by acts of heroism.

Newspaper reporter
In general all people who were independent or who stuck to their own opinions were roughly handled or put aside when the time came for favours. You could be boycotted; you could be driven out of business. These things were noticed by most people, who learned from the fate of others.

C The bomb plot fails

On 20 July between five and six o'clock in the afternoon Haeften telephoned and told me to come at once. 'We're taking over,' he said . . . .

For the time being there was nothing I could do except hang around and observe. In spite of the apparent turmoil, all I heard and saw, particularly snatches of Stauffenberg's telephone calls, gave me the impression that the whole Army was up in arms against the Nazis. It never occurred to me at that moment that they could reverse the process and stop everything . . . . So I believed our cause was really won. I had little doubt that Himmler would try to put up some resistance through the SS, but I was sure Hitler was dead and that I could trust the resolution of the generals and the loyalty of their officers and men . . . . I went home to tell my brother what I believed had happened at Rastenburg.

When I got there, I found my brother with Claus Bonhoeffer. We opened a bottle of champagne to drink to the glorious future. We were too excited to sleep, and stayed up drinking champagne. We had the radio on, waiting for further news. The continuous recital of military music which had been going on all evening worried me slightly; I wondered why it was that we had not yet taken over the broadcasting stations. Then around one o'clock, Hitler spoke . . . .

From R. Manvell and H. Fraenkel, *The July Plot*, London, 1964.

Questions

1 Look at the groups Kessler thought would rise up and resist Hitler (Source A). What difficulties would the organiser of such resistance face?

2 What difficulty would historians have in understanding the situation in Germany if they only had diaries such as this to work from?

3 What three reasons were given by the inhabitants of Northeim for the lack of resistance in their town?

4 Do you think these people were right in their attitudes? How do you imagine you and your family would have acted? (Refer to Unit 38.)

5 Why was Otto John so sure that 'our cause was really won' (Source C)?

6 How does Source C show the important role played by the radio in this and other events of the time?

7 Describe the thoughts that must have raced through Otto's mind as he heard Hitler's voice on the radio in the early hours of 21 July.

Part 8

Hitler and the European War

40 Hitler's foreign policy goals

German attitudes towards other countries in the 1920s and 1930s were dominated by feelings of bitterness toward the Treaty of Versailles. In her autobiography, written in the 1950s, Melita Maschmann recalls how, as a child, her mother had constantly reminded her of how badly Germany had been treated (Source B).

When Hitler came to power in 1933 he promised to 'smash' the treaty. He also played upon German fears and hopes, as the two posters from a Nazi exhibition held in the 1940s show (Sources A and C).

A   German fears: the Empire before 1933

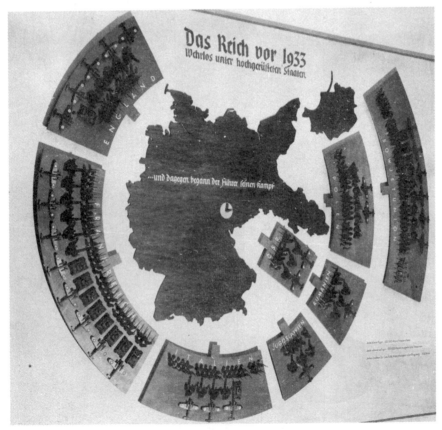

'Defenceless before other "high-riding" states . . . and against this the leader began his struggle.'

B A German mother's view

Countless times she impressed upon us that Germany had lost the war, although no nation had braver soldiers. Her lands had been carved up on every side in a shameful, dictated peace, her economy was in decline, thanks to the reparation payments demanded by the former enemy countries. Her culture was dominated by foreigners. She was mortally sick.

From M. Maschmann, *Account Rendered* (trans. G. Strachen), Abelard-Schuman, 1964.

C The return of the German peoples

'Those from the old German Empire return home.'

Questions

1 On what traditional German fear does Source A play?

2 How does this poster suggest that the peace treaty contributes to this fear?

3 Which of Hitler's actions which broke the terms of the peace treaty does this poster try to justify?

4 Is 'carved up' a fair way of explaining what happened to German territory at the Treaty of Versailles? Explain.

5 If your parents were constantly talking to you in this way about the state of Britain, how might you react?

6 Look back at the Nazi Party Programme of 1920 (Unit 8). To which point does Source C refer?

7 How did this goal fit in with Hitler's racial theories?

41 The Czech crisis, September 1938

In the summer of 1938 the Czech people knew that Hitler had laid claim to the Sudetenland, the part of their country where 3.25 million German-speaking Czechs lived. What would Britain and France do? France was Czechoslovakia's ally and Britain was bound by the Treaty of Locarno to back France. Up to the summer of 1938 the Czechs had not resisted Hitler's moves. Only that spring he had ignored the Treaty of Versailles and taken over Austria. Just before this 'Anschluss' David Low, the cartoonist with the Evening Standard, *mocked the British and French response to Germany's action (Source A).*

William Shirer, an American journalist, was in Berlin throughout the Czech crisis. His diary for 26 September shows how near war seemed (Source B). Then Britain, France and Italy held a conference with Hitler at Munich without consulting Czechoslovakia. Hitler could have the Sudetenland in return for agreeing to 'Peace for our time'. This news was broadcast to the Czech people by their Premier, General Syrový (Source C). Eric Gedye was the Daily Telegraph's *correspondent in Austria and Czechoslovakia. He had been sickened by what he had witnessed after the Nazi take-over of Austria and now he felt ashamed to be British (Source D).*

A 'Increasing the pressure'

From the *Evening Standard*, 18 February 1938.

B Nearly at war, 26 September

Hitler had finally burned his last bridges. Shouting and shrieking in the worst state of excitement I've ever seen him in, he stated in the Sportplatz tonight that he would have his Sudetenland by October 1 – next Saturday, today being Monday. If Beneš [the Czech President] doesn't hand it over to him he will go to war, this Saturday . . . . Twice Hitler screamed that this is absolutely his last territorial demand in Europe. Speaking of his assurances to Chamberlain [the British Prime Minister], he said: 'I further assured him that when the Czechs have reconciled themselves with their minorities, the Czech state no longer interests me.'

From W. L. Shirer, *Berlin Diary 1934–41*, Sphere, 1970.

C The Czechs' dilemma, 30 September 1938

. . . In Munich, four Great Powers met together and decided to demand of us the acceptance of new frontiers which separate the German-speaking areas from our State. They confronted us with the choice between a desperate and hopeless defence which would have meant the sacrifice of the whole younger generation, their wives and their children, and the acceptance of the conditions forced upon us . . . . We were abandoned. We stand alone.

From G. E. R. Gedye, *Fallen Bastions*, Gollancz, 1939.

D Nazis enter the Sudetenland, October 1939

The whole horrible drama [of Nazi Occupation] is today being re-enacted in the Sudeten areas. This time you must not blame Hitler so much. He has three colleagues . . . . Plunder, murder, insult, torture, concentration camps, ruined existences, head-hunting, refusal of asylum* by the Czechs and brutal handing over of refugees to the Nazis – 'individually responsible' are these four Powers, excluding Czechoslovakia but including Britain.

Does that disturb your sleep?

From G. E. R. Gedye, *Fallen Bastions*, Gollancz, 1939.

* *place of safety*

Questions

1 How does Low make fun of the British and the French?

2 What three devices does he use to show Germany as the aggressive power?

3 Britain is shown as putting all her eggs in one basket. What policy does this basket represent? Is it true that *all* Britain's 'eggs' were in it?

4 Do the reassurances given to Britain in Hitler's speech make the cartoon seem unfair to Germany?

5 How does the Czech Premier show that his government felt betrayed by the Munich Agreement?

6 Who does Gedye mean by Hitler's three colleagues? Is he making a fair comment?

42 Steps to war, 1938–39

On 10 November 1938 Hitler spoke to a secret press conference for 400 German journalists. There, he shattered any belief that the Munich Conference was meant to bring peace (Source A).

In March 1939 Hitler's armies invaded the rest of Czechoslovakia. Britain and France abandoned appeasement and gave a guarantee to stand by Poland if she were attacked. Hitler's reply was to open secret talks with the USSR and to sign a pact with her on 23 August. William Shirer, the American journalist, recorded his thoughts on the Nazi-Soviet Pact (Source B). Two days later Hitler told the British Ambassador, Sir Nevile Henderson, why he wanted the Pact (Source C).

On 1 September Germany invaded Poland and two days later Britain declared war. Paul Schmidt, Hitler's interpreter, later recalled how Hitler received the British ultimatum (Source D), while William Shirer describes how people reacted to the news that they were at war (Source E).

A Hitler explains his policies, November 1938

For years circumstances have compelled me to talk about almost nothing but peace. Only by continually stressing Germany's desire for peace and her peaceful intentions could I achieve freedom for the German people bit by bit and provide the armaments which were always necessary before the next steps could be taken. It is obvious that such peace propaganda also has its doubtful aspects, for it can only too easily give people the idea that the present regime really identifies itself with the determination to preserve peace at all costs. That would not only lead to a wrong assessment of the aims of this system, but above all it might lead to the German nation, instead of being prepared for every eventuality, being filled with a spirit of defeatism . . . .

From J. Noakes and G. Pridham, *Documents on Nazism*, Jonathan Cape, 1974.

B The Nazi-Soviet Pact, 23 August 1938

Great excitement at the Taverne tonight. About two a.m. we get the terms of the Russian-German Pact. It goes much further than anyone dreamed. It's a virtual alliance and Stalin, the supposed arch-enemy of Nazism and aggressor, by its terms invites Germany to go in and clean up Poland. The friends of the Bolos* are consternated . . . . Will a French Communist, say, who has been taught for six years to hate Nazism above all else, swallow Moscow's embracing of Hitler? Maybe, though, Stalin is smart. His aim: to bring on a war between Germany and the West which will result in chaos, after which the Bolsheviks step in . . . .

From W. L. Shirer, *Berlin Diary 1934–41*, Sphere, 1970.

* *Bolsheviks*

C Hitler and Henderson: no war on two fronts

In contrast to the last war Germany would no longer have to fight on two fronts. Agreement with Russia was unconditional and signified a change in foreign policy of the Reich [which would] last a very long time. Russia and Germany would never again take up arms against each other.

From *British Foreign Policy . . . 1919–1939*, HMSO, 1954.

D Paul Schmidt delivers the ultimatum

When I entered the next room Hitler was sitting at his desk and Ribbentrop* stood by the window. Both looked up expectantly as I came in. I stopped at some distance from Hitler's desk, and then slowly translated the British Government's ultimatum. When I finished, there was complete silence.

Hitler sat motionless, gazing before him. He was not at a loss, as was afterwards stated, nor did he rage, as others allege. He sat completely silent and unmoving . . . . In the ante-room also this news was followed by complete silence.

From J. Noakes and G. Pridham, *Documents on Nazism*, Jonathan Cape, 1974.

* *Nazi foreign minister*

E Berlin at war, 3 September

I was standing in the Wilhelmplatz about noon when the loud-speakers suddenly announced that England had declared herself at war with Germany. Some 250 people were standing there in the sun. They listened attentively to the announcement. When it was finished, there was not a murmur. They just stood there as they were before. Stunned . . . no excitement, no hurrahs, no cheering, no throwing of flowers, no war fever, no war hysteria.

From W. L. Shirer, *Berlin Diary 1934–41*, Sphere, 1970.

Questions

1 What does Hitler see as (a) the advantages; (b) the disadvantages of having been forced to talk of peace (Source A)?

2 Pick out *two* statements which show that Hitler was not very interested in peace.

3 What do you think Hitler expected these journalists to do after this press conference?

4 From Source B, explain why 'the friends of the Bolos' would be 'consternated'.

5 Do you find Shirer's explanation of Stalin's sudden friendship with Hitler convincing?

6 What do you think was Hitler's aim in his talk with the British Ambassador?

7 How would you explain Hitler's behaviour on receiving the ultimatum?

8 What other occasion might William Shirer have been thinking about when he wrote his diary entry?

43 The German war economy

Source A is an anti-Nazi cartoon which comments on the German take-over of the Skoda arms works in Czechoslovakia.

Hitler refused to conscript German women. Instead, his government tried to attract foreign workers to Germany. Source B gives some idea of how they were treated and by 1940 it was clear that this would not solve the shortage. In the next five years millions of people were deported to Germany as slave labour from occupied Europe. Meanwhile, the inmates of concentration camps were systematically worked to death. In Source C Albert Speer, minister in charge of the war effort, describes a camp where V2 rockets were made, in his memoirs written during his twenty years in prison for war crimes. Nazi censorship makes it difficult to judge how ordinary Germans reacted to the war effort but Sources D and E suggest there was a lot of grumbling.

A 'Labour organisation in the Skoda factory'

B 'Duties of male and female civilian workers of Polish nationality'

1 It is strictly forbidden to leave the place of residence.
2 Public conveyances, such as railways, may be used only after special consent ....
3 Every Polish male and female worker must always wear visibly the badge issued ....
4 Anyone who shirks his work ... will be transferred to a concentration camp ....

From J. Noakes and G. Pridham, *Documents on Nazism*, Jonathan Cape, 1974.

100

C Albert Speer visits an armaments labour camp

I inspected the extensive underground installations where the V-2 was to be produced. In enormous long halls prisoners were busy setting up machinery and shifting plumbing. Expressionlessly, they looked right through me, mechanically removing their prisoners' caps of blue twill until our group had passed them . . . .

The conditions for these prisoners were in fact barbarous, and a sense of profound involvement and personal guilt seizes me whenever I think of them. As I learned from the overseers after the inspection was over, the sanitary conditions were inadequate, disease rampant; the prisoners were quartered right there in the damp caves, and as a result the mortality among them was extraordinarily high . . . .

From A. Speer, Inside the Third Reich, Sphere, 1975.

D Local Government report from a rural area, 1941

We've victories enough already. Now we need peace. That, briefly put, is the feeling among the greatest part of the population. This longing for peace is probably partly based in the difficulties of getting provisions and in restrictions which in a long war are felt to be ever more burdensome. Mostly . . . it is rooted in the noticeable shortage of labour. The father, the husband, or the son have been away from the farm all too long.

From I. Kershaw, Popular Opinion and Political Dissent in the Third Reich, Clarendon Press, 1983.

E Regional report, May 1943

Business people of every kind openly curse the NSDAP and its leaders. 'I didn't vote for Hitler!' has become a sort of catchphrase among business people.

From I. Kershaw, Popular Opinion and Political Dissent in the Third Reich, Clarendon Press, 1983.

Questions

1 What stereotype of the Nazis is presented in Source A?

2 To what kind of life did this list of rules (Source B), if seriously enforced, reduce the foreign workers?

3 What Nazi attitudes or beliefs do these rules reveal? Take one example.

4 What made Speer talk of 'personal guilt'

5 Speer tells us he was unaware of the brutal treatment of camp workers. Give reasons (a) why this might have been so, (b) why this was unlikely.

6 Although the content of the complaints mentioned in Sources D and E is not that shocking, their existence in official documents is surprising. Why?

44 The Jewish tragedy

Sources A, B, C and D are accounts of mass murder. They are not the most terrible documents about the holocaust but they are appalling enough. As you read them, respect the memory of 6 million people who were deliberately murdered on our continent forty years ago. Think too of the few survivors and of the millions of relatives and friends of the victims all over the world who have to live with the pain of knowing from accounts such as these what was done to their loved ones.

You will not be able to avoid asking yourself why it happened, could it happen again and how a nation – any nation – could cross the lines which separate small acts of prejudice from vicious persecution and then murder. Is the lesson that these lines do not exist and that these evils cannot be separated?

Milton Wynne (Source A) was one of the young American GIs who liberated the death camps in 1945. What he saw horrified him beyond belief; in his poems, written at the time, he tried to understand the Jewish experience. Here he considers what it must have been like to be on one of the dreaded transport trains.

Tadeusz Borowski (Source B) was a young Polish Communist prisoner in Auschwitz from 1943–45. One of his duties had been to meet those transport trains. After the war he wrote some short stories about life in the camp: he was determined to be brutally frank, to leave nothing out, however painful the memory.

Primo Levi (Source C) was a young Italian Jewish chemist who was brought to Auschwitz in 1944. Out of his transport of 650 men, women and children only three survived. As one of those survivors, Levi felt duty-bound to write his auto-biography after the war to bear witness to the way that Auschwitz had tried to turn the inmates into beasts. He describes how he felt once he had gone through the degrading process of becoming an inmate: being left naked for hours, shaved, tattooed and dressed in lice-ridden pyjamas and wooden clogs.

In the early 1960s a Frankfurt judge and jury visited the remains of Auschwitz. A former camp doctor and nineteen SS men were on trial. Amos Elon a former Auschwitz prisoner, went with them through the camp (Source D).

A Milton Wynne

Did you ever ride in a European freight car?
I did.
We went for 24 hours in a boxcar filled up with
40 of us.
We had cases of C rations.
We had water.
We had two blankets each.
We even were able to make a fire to keep warm.
At night we huddled together and pooled the blankets.
And still got up stiff and cold and sleepless the next morning.
When we all stood up
there was enough room to walk about a little.
At the end of 24 hours we had learned how to urinate out the door as
the train rushed on, with the wind – so it wouldn't
sweep back into the car.

From M. Wynne, *Why I Hate the Nazis*, Aca Gallery, NY, 1945.

We had learned to kill time by looking out the door, or
dozing on the floor.
And when we got out of that car at the end of 24 hours, we were a
bunch of rugged guys.
It was a rough ride that had cut into us and we didn't like it.

Well, I hear that Jews went for little excursions like that pretty often.
Only with some variations.
Their cars were jammed so full that they couldn't even sit down.
There were no blankets, no fire, no food, no water, no opening of doors for relief;
only the rhythm of the wheels, the moaning of the sick and dying, the filth and
the smell, the hunger and the cold, AND THE COLD AND THE COLD
and the single thought that the gas piped into the car would soon put an end
to the whole works.

B Tadeusz Borowski

'The transport is coming,' somebody says. We spring to our feet, all
eyes turn in one direction. Around the bend, one after another, the
cattle cars begin rolling in. The train backs into the station, a
conductor leans out, waves his hand, blows a whistle. The locomotive
whistles back with a shrieking noise, puffs, the train rolls slowly alongside the ramp. In the tiny barred windows appear pale, wilted,
exhausted human faces, terror-stricken women with tangled hair,
unshaven men. They gaze at the station in silence. And then, suddenly,
there is a stir in the cars and a pounding against the wooden boards.
  'Water! Air!' – weary, desperate cries.
  Heads push through windows, mouths gasp frantically for air. They
draw a few breaths, then disappear; others come in their place, then
also disappear. The cries and moans grow louder . . . .
  The bolts crack, the doors fall open. A wave of fresh air rushes inside
the train. People . . . inhumanly crammed buried under incredible
heaps of luggage . . . Monstrously squeezed together, they have fainted
from heat, suffocated, crushed one another. Now they push towards
the opened doors . . . .
  But before they have a chance to recover, before they can draw a
breath of fresh air and look at the sky, bundles are snatched from their
hands, coats ripped off their backs, their purses and umbrellas taken
away . . . . A woman reaches down quickly to pick up her handbag.
The whip flies, the woman screams, stumbles, and falls under the feet
of the surging crowd. Behind her, a child cries in a thin little voice
'Mamele!' – a very small girl with tangled black curls . . . .
  Trucks, loaded with people, start up with a deafening roar and drive
off amidst the wailing and screaming of the women separated from
their children, and the stupefied silence of the men left behind. They
are the ones who had been ordered to step to the right – the healthy
and the young who will go to the camp. In the end, they too will not
escape death, but first they must work . . . .

From Tadeusz
Borowski, *This Way for
the Gas, Ladies and
Gentlemen* (trans. B.
Vedder), Penguin, 1976.

C Primo Levi

Here I am then, on the bottom. One learns quickly enough to wipe out the past and the future when one is forced to. A fortnight after my arrival I already had the prescribed hunger, that chronic hunger unknown to free men, which makes one dream at night, and settles in all the limbs of one's body. I have already learnt not to let myself be robbed, and in fact if I find a spoon lying around, a piece of string, a button which I can acquire without danger of punishment, I pocket them and consider them mine by full right. On the back of my feet I already have those numb sores that will not heal. I push wagons, I work with a shovel, I turn rotten in the rain, I shiver in the wind; already my body is no longer mine; my belly is swollen, my limbs emaciated, my face is thick in the morning, hollow in the evening, some of us have yellow skin, others grey. When we do not meet for a few days we hardly recognise each other.

We Italians had decided to meet every Sunday evening in a corner of the lager*, but we stopped it at once, because it was too sad to count our numbers and find fewer each time, and to see each other ever more deformed and more squalid. And it was so tiring to walk those few steps – then, meeting each other, to remember and to think. It was better not to think.

From Primo Levi, *If this is a Man* (trans. Stuart Woolf), Bodley Head, 1966.

(or laager) an encircled camp.

D Amos Elon

The court moves along. Here is a cellar, Penal Barracks 11. A great deal has been heard about it in the Frankfurt courtroom. Witnesses testify and with tear-choked voices have fainted from the violence of their recollections, have come to again and continued to testify. It is dark and damp in the cellar. The crowd peers into a dungeon, barely three by three yards wide, with a tiny hatch. Here, 40 people were stuffed together without food. They struggled for air, screamed, starved to death and suffocated .... Their crimes recorded meticulously:

From Amos Elon, *Journey through a Haunted Land* (trans. M. Roloff) Andre Deutsch, 1967.

Prisoner 64,166 admitted May, 1943; he allowed a tool to drop to the ground, the handle bent.

Prisoner 42,658 admitted March 14, 1943; he had tried to obtain a second bowl of soup.

Prisoner 64,495 admitted June 5, 1943; he had relieved himself on the job.

At the main gate, below the cast iron band with the inscription, 'Arbeit Macht Frei'* small talk cuts into the general silence .... The court is in a hurry. Now it stands in front of the 'Black Wall'. Some 20,000 people were murdered here. Naked, running in double-time, they came out of the penal bunkers to the right. Kapos flung them against the wall. A single shot in the nape of the neck. The blood flowed into the gutter.

work brings freedom

Judge Hotz gives the sign for everyone to depart. The inspection is at an end. The court returns to the base camp, Auschwitz I. Here, the Polish government has converted some former prison barracks into a museum. The barracks are heated now, there are curtains strung over windows blocked by rusty bars, even doormats at the entrance . . . . And yet it is here that the sober, matter-of-fact façade of the jurors suddenly disintegrates. The Judge bursts into tears. He stands with his staff before the remains of the murdered; whole rooms filled with children's shoes, spectacles, crutches, prayer books, valises, men's suits, dresses, dentures. Thousands of toothbrushes, mountains upon mountains of women's hair, cut prior to gassing, some still in sacks labelled for shipping to a firm in Bavaria that manufactured insulating material for submarines.

45 The War is lost, 1945

By March 1945 the Allies were closing in all around Germany – the Americans and British from the west and the Russians from the east. Albert Speer was Minister for Munitions and Armaments at the time. His memoirs, written in prison after the war, show how serious Germany's military position was and how, despite this, some Germans still had faith in their Fuehrer (Source A).

Hitler spent the closing stages of the war deep underground in a concrete bunker below the Reich Chancellery in Berlin. Here, Speer visited him regularly and observed how his physical condition worsened and how he was increasingly out of touch with military realities (Source B).

One of Hitler's last acts was to issue the destruction order of 19 March 1945 (Source C). In his memoirs Speer also recalls his last visit to Hitler's bunker, just one week before Hitler, Eva Braun (his mistress) and the Goebbels family committed suicide rather than surrender to the Russians (Source D).

A Speer on the situation, March 1945

I had returned to Berlin on March 21. Early in the morning three days later I received the news that British troops had crossed the Rhine on a broad front, north of the Ruhr, without meeting any resistance. Our troops were helpless .... As late as September 1944 our strenuous production of armaments had made it possible to erect a new defensive front in a short time out of weaponless armies. This could no longer be done. Germany was being overrun.

I drove to the Ruhr area once more. Saving its industry was the crucial question for the post-war era. In Westphalia a flat tyre forced us to stop. Unrecognised in the twilight, I stood in a farmyard talking to the farmers. To my surprise, the faith in Hitler which had been hammered into their minds all these last years was still strong. Hitler could never lose the war, they declared. 'The Fuehrer is still holding something in reserve that he'll play at the last moment. It's only a trap, his letting the enemy come so far into our country.'

From A. Speer, *Inside the Third Reich*, Sphere, 1975.

B Speer on Hitler in March 1945

He was shrivelling up like an old man. His limbs trembled; he walked stooped, with dragging footsteps. Even his voice became quavering and lost its old masterfulness. Its force had given way to a faltering, toneless manner of speaking. When he became excited, as he frequently did in a senile way, his voice would start breaking. He still had his fits of obstinacy, but they no longer reminded one of a child's temper tantrums, but of an old man's. His complexion was sallow, his face swollen; his uniform, which in the past he had kept scrupulously neat, was often neglected in this last period of life and stained by food he had eaten with a shaking hand ....

From A. Speer, *Inside the Third Reich*, Sphere, 1975.

Even in the situation conferences at the beginning of April, Hitler was still talking about counter-operations, about attacks upon the Western enemy's exposed flanks – the Allied troops were now beyond Kassel and moving forward at a swift pace toward Eisenach, Hitler continued to send his divisions from one place to another – a cruel phantom war game. For when I would come back from a visit to the front and check the previous day's movements of our troops on the map, I could only note that I had seen nothing of them in the region I had driven through – and what troops I had passed consisted of soldiers without heavy weapons armed solely with rifles . . . nothing was said about evacuations and retreats.

C Hitler's destruction order, 19 March 1945

The fight for the existence of our nation compels us to exploit all means, even within the Reich, which can weaken the enemy's fighting capacity and impede his further progress . . . .

> I therefore order:
>> 1. All military, transport, communication, industrial, and supply installations as well as equipment within the Reich which the enemy might use for the continuation of his struggle now or in the future must be destroyed . . . .

From J. Noakes and G. Pridham, *Documents on Nazism*, Jonathan Cape, 1974.

D Speer's last visit to the bunker, 23 April

Rather apathetically, wearily and as if it were already a matter of course, he began speaking of his death: 'I too have resolved to stay here . . . . I shall not fight personally. There is always the danger that I would only be wounded and fall into the hands of the Russians alive. I don't want my enemies to disgrace my body either. I've given orders that I be cremated. Fräulein Braun wants to depart this life with me, and I'll shoot Blondi* beforehand . . . .'

She [Eva Braun] was the only prominent candidate for death in this bunker who displayed an admirable and superior composure. While all the others were abnormal – exaltedly heroic like Goebbels, bent on saving his skin like Bormann, exhausted like Hitler, or in total collapse like Frau Goebbels – Eva Braun radiated an almost gay serenity. 'How about a bottle of champagne for our farewell? And some sweets? I'm sure you haven't eaten in a long time.'

From A. Speer, *Inside the Third Reich*, Sphere, 1975.

*his dog.

Questions

1 How does Speer see the British crossing of the Rhine as bad news for Germany?

2 Why does he use the word 'hammered' in Source A?

3 How do you imagine the farmers in Source A would have reacted if they had seen the Hitler that Speer describes in Source B?

4 What evidence is there in Source B to support Speer's view in Source A that the German armies were now 'helpless'?

5 How can you tell that Hitler's staff in the bunker were helping him in his 'phantom' war games? What reasons might they have had for doing this?

6 Why would the farmers' faith in Hitler have been utterly shattered if they had been aware of the destruction order in March 1945?

7 How can you tell from Source B that Speer was totally opposed to this order?

8 How does Hitler reveal a completely unrealistic outlook in his alleged conversation with Speer in Source D?

9 Do you think Hitler was right to worry about his body being disgraced after his death? Explain.

10 How can you tell that the Nazi leaders had a comfortable lifestyle in the bunker, and what would the farmers in Source A have had to say about that?

46 The Nazi legacy: a stunned survivor looks back

On 8 May 1945 the German armies surrendered unconditionally. Germany was in a state of total collapse. All her cities were in ruins, her population was half starving, millions of refugees choked her roads, and she had no government. Source A is a photograph of one city taken in 1945.

Many Germans had suffered at the hands of the Nazis and for them 8 May was a day of liberation, but they were the minority. The Allies soon rounded up some 22,000 Nazis. The most famous were put on trial at Nuremberg. Melita Maschmann was one of the thousands of anonymous party workers tried and imprisoned out of the public glare. Afterwards she wrote a book in the form of a letter to a school friend, a Jewish girl who disappeared under Hitler, explaining how she became 'a dedicated, unfeeling Nazi'. In Source B she describes the refugees she helped when fleeing from the Russians. Then, she talks of the sense of loss when she first became aware of the emptiness of Nazism (Source C). Towards the end of her book she tries to summarise what was evil about Nazism (Source D).

A A German city in 1945

B Melita Maschmann: kindness among refugees

There were two brothers amongst the children, one about seven and the other a little boy of two. The elder brother fought for the little one like a mother for her child. I came across the two of them later in a refugee camp. I watched the elder brother stealing a sausage from a sack, biting it into pieces and pushing it bit by bit into his brother's mouth. Believe me, I saw more people helping one another during the last months of the war than ever before or since. Everywhere I met people who had left all they had behind them because the war had taken away their homes, their belongings and often their families as well.

From M. Maschmann, *Account Rendered* (trans. G. Strachen), Abelard-Schuman, 1964.

C A Nazi's despair

The despair which had overtaken me on the first day of my solitary confinement in Heidelberg prison was now to become my dominant mood for years ... despair at the pointlessness of all our experiences. During the period of the Third Reich we were spoilt by a sense of the significance of our existence which affected almost every activity. If we ate a piece of bread we could believe we were strengthening ourselves for the fight for a German victory. If we decided not to eat the bread, we could believe that it would fortify for the struggle someone else whose need was greater than ours. Now both things seemed equally pointless . . . .

From M. Maschmann, *Account Rendered* (trans. G. Strachen), Abelard-Schuman, 1964.

D Serving evil

You know that I became a National Socialist because the idea of the National Community inspired me. What I had never realised was the number of Germans who were not considered worthy to belong to this community . . . . No one is proof against making political error at any time, but wherever one is concerned with people living together – and politics also covers this – there is always a simple commandment and with it a yardstick: human kindness. Where it is sinned against callously, the politics are wrong . . . . My friends are kindly people . . . they would also like to forgive. But I believe that they feel they have no power to grant the absolution to which their hearts may urge them, to one person or another. The dead at their backs are too powerful because of their awesome numbers . . . . The ghastly thing was just the fact that it was not gangsters and roughnecks, but decent, intelligent and moral people who allowed themselves to be induced to acquiesce* in something deeply evil and to serve it . . . . Even a person of particular integrity and kindliness can be induced by fanaticism to evil, because the fanatic believes that the end justifies the means.

From M. Maschmann, *Account Rendered* (trans. G. Strachen), Abelard-Schuman, 1964.

* show acceptance

Questions

1 What is a refugee? How does Source A help explain the huge numbers of refugees in Germany in 1945?

2 Has anyone you know, who has lived through a war or a similar crisis, got a story to tell about how people manage to cope?

3 What reasons might the Allies have had for keeping the arrested Nazis in cells on their own?

4 Can you explain in your own words what Melita Maschmann means by 'a sense of the significance of our existence' in Source C?

5 From Source D how would you describe the main lesson that Melita Maschmann seems to have learned from her experience of being a Nazi?

6 What danger is she trying to draw our attention to when she talks of those who believe that 'the end justifies the means'?

For discussion

7 Imagine that you had found that your parents had been active Nazis. What questions would you want to put to them?

8 How could such a terrible thing as the Third Reich happen?

Acknowledgements

We are grateful to the following for permission to reproduce copyright material:

Blackie & Son Ltd for extracts from *Account Rendered* by M. Maschmann; The Bodley Head/The Putnam Publishing Group for abridged extracts from *The July Plot* by R. Manvell & Heinrich Frankel. Copyright © 1964 by Hennerton Productions Inc. & Heinrich Frankel; Constable & Co. Ltd/E. P. Dutton Inc. for extracts from *An English Wife in Berlin* by Princess E. Bluecher; Andre Deutsch Ltd for extracts from *Journey through a Haunted Land* by Amos Elon, trans. M. Roloff (1967); Hodder & Stoughton Ltd for abridged extracts from *Memoirs of a Social Democrat* Vol II (1929) by Philip Scheidemann, trans. J. E. Michell; Authors' Agents on behalf of the Authors for extracts in translation from *Documents on Nazism* by Jeremy Noakes & Geoffrey Pridham, pubd. Jonathan Cape Ltd; Penguin Books Ltd/Geisenheyner & Crone for extracts from *This way to the Gas, Ladies and Gentlemen* by Tadeusz Browski, trans. Barbara Vedder (Penguin Books 1976). Copyright © Maria Borowski 1959. Trans. Copyright © Penguin Books Ltd 1967; Charles Scribner's Sons, an inprint of Macmillan Pubg Co. for extracts from *I Knew Hitler* by Kurt G. W. Ludecke. Copyright 1937 Kurt G. W. Ludecke. Copyright renewed © 1965 Kurt G. W. Ludecke; George Weidenfeld & Nicholson Ltd for abridged extracts from *Inside the Third Reich* (1971) by Albert Speer.

We have unfortunately been unable to trace the copyright owners of the poem 'Why I Hate the Nazis' by Corporal M. Wynne and would appreciate any information which would enable us to do so.

We are grateful to the following for permission to reproduce photographs: L. Brandt, page 51; Bundesarchiv, Koblenz, pages 50, 73, 109; *Daily Express*, page 64; Imperial War Museum, London, pages 8, 11, 36; Library of Congress, pages 33, 39, 43, 44, 48, 80, 85, 94, 95; *Punch*, 5, 14, 17, 20, 63; Solo Syndication, London, pages 71, 96; Ullstein Bilderdienst, page 69; Weidenfeld & Nicolson for cartoon from *The Diaries of a Cosmopolitan, Count Harry Kessler, 1918–1937*, translated and edited by Charles Kessler, page 55; Wiener Library, London, pages 75, 83. We are unable to trace the copyright holder for photos on pages 77, 100 and would appreciate receiving any information that would enable us to do so.